Every page in this book is a testament to the most powerful weapon we have as believers in a dark and hostile world—love. While many have written about life in the inner city where violence and crime are everyday occurrences, Pastor Choco has lived this and come out on the other side, more determined than ever to combat every enemy of peace with love, hope, and the profound message of grace, mercy, and salvation.

—Jentezen Franklin
Senior Pastor, Free Chapel
New York Times Best-Selling Author

My covenant brother for close to thirty years, Pastor Choco's love for the marginalized serves as a modern-day unbridled application of the Good Samaritan parable. His leadership transformed Chicago, and now his message stands poised to change the world. Beyond a must read, this is a must do!

—Pastor Samuel Rodriguez
President, National Hispanic Christian
Leadership Conference

Jesus told us that the world will know we are His followers because of our love. Yet how many of us are living lives that demonstrate His love in such a way that people we encounter are drawn to Him? This is the challenge Pastor Choco presents to us in *Love Them Anyway*, a challenge that, if met, can truly change the world one person at a time. Read this book and use it as a catalyst for change in your own heart and mind, transforming you into a living, breathing extension of God's love to others.

—Mark Batterson
New York Times Best-Selling Author, *The Circle Maker*
Lead Pastor, National

Few men model a life of love, humility, and service like Pastor Choco De Jesús. Upon the foundation of these virtues, he built and led one of the largest and fastest-growing churches in America. Many people want to know the secret to his success. I believe his new book, *Love Them Anyway*, provides the answer. It is a must read for every Christian who wants to learn to love like Jesus. It contains the remedy for the climate of division that plagues the church today. It's a powerful and timely word. I highly recommend *Love Them Anyway* and the ministry of Wilfredo "Choco" De Jesús.

—EVANGELIST DANIEL KOLENDA
PRESIDENT AND CEO, CHRIST FOR ALL NATIONS

Our world has never been in more desperate need of unity and respect for people of all walks of life. Jesus modeled this kind of love for us, and we must take up the mantle and share His pure, unadulterated love with everyone we meet. Only then will we see divisions healed and lives transformed. I commend Pastor Choco for not only writing this book but living its message every day as a powerful witness of the difference one person's life can make when we choose to *love them anyway.*

—JOHN HANNAH
FOUNDER AND LEAD PASTOR, NEW LIFE COVENANT
CHURCH SOUTHEAST
AUTHOR, *DESPERATE FOR JESUS*

LOVE
THEM
ANYWAY

LOVE
THEM
ANYWAY

CHOCO DE JESÚS, EdD

CHARISMA HOUSE

Most Charisma House Book Group products are available at special quantity discounts for bulk purchase for sales promotions, premiums, fund-raising, and educational needs. For details, call us at (407) 333-0600 or visit our website at www.charismahouse.com.

Love Them Anyway by Wilfredo "Choco" De Jesús
Published by Charisma House
Charisma Media/Charisma House Book Group
600 Rinehart Road, Lake Mary, Florida 32746

Visit the author's website at www.lovethembook.com.

Library of Congress Cataloging-in-Publication Data:
An application to register this book for cataloging has been submitted to the Library of Congress.
International Standard Book Number: 978-1-62999-715-5
E-book ISBN: 978-1-62999-716-2

Some of the stories in this book have appeared in different form in *Amazing Faith*, ISBN 978-1-93669-995-7, copyright © 2012;

In the Gap, ISBN 978-1-93830-989-2, copyright © 2014; and
Stay the Course, ISBN 978-0-99733-722-8, copyright © 2016.

21 22 23 24 25 — 9 8 7 6 5 4 3 2 1
Printed in the United States of America

I dedicate this book to everyone who has felt overlooked, rejected, or betrayed by the church. If I'm the offender—if I didn't take the time to listen to you, engage with you, and show you the love of Jesus—please forgive me. I'm still growing and learning. I look forward to meaningful, respectful conversations with people who have beliefs that are different from mine.

CONTENTS

ACKNOWLEDGMENTS

I WANT TO SAY thank you to my Lord and Savior for the greatest example in displaying love. Thank you to the disciples for carrying that mantle, to all those who have been imprisoned and martyred for this love. To Christians who are asking the prevailing question, "What do we do now?" I say, "Love them!"

I want to thank Charisma House for believing in me, especially Steve Strang and Marcos Perez for believing in this message and in my ability to communicate it and for pushing this book forward. I also want to thank Pat Springle for capturing my thoughts and my heart. I want to thank Susan and Steve Blount for being a bridge and facilitating the networking process. Thank you, New Life Covenant, for allowing me to grow in this love and helping me display it in crazy ways in Chicago. To the Assemblies of God, I want to express my gratitude for the confidence you have placed in me. My heart is to serve and to be of encouragement to our fellowship.

To my tireless wife, Elizabeth, who has been with me and always believes in me, thank you for helping me put my words down in ways that people can read them and be inspired. To my children, whom I love so much, keep the love alive in your lives and ministry. Papi is so proud of you, Alex and Anthony, Yesenia and Anders, Pito and Eden. To my two granddaughters, Charlie Grace and Reagan Liv, I love you girls. You have given me and your mama a brand-new love. To my grandsons, James Anthony and Donovan Ray, I love you boys and look forward to teaching you about this love of Jesus. To Sky, can't wait to see your face. Papa will love you the same.

FOREWORD

I LOVE THE CHURCH. I was born into a pastor's home. My teeth were cut on the back of church pews. When my father passed away unexpectedly when I was only nine years old, it would have been easy to feel abandoned, lonely, or somehow cheated. I didn't.

The reason I didn't feel abandoned is because I was part of a vibrant church community that knew how to show love—real love—to those inside and outside of their circle of influence. Men from our church would take me to Detroit Tigers games. They would come and see my ball games. They would take me on campouts. They rallied around me and, in a spiritual sense, became like fathers to me.

It should be no surprise that a healthy, Spirit-empowered church would be outgoing in its demonstration of love. After all, the apostle Paul described love as a fruit (or evidence) of the Holy Spirit at work in our lives.

Two researchers at the University of California—Berkeley set out to see how Christians engage in compassionate relief in a global context. They quickly saw the outsized impact of the Pentecostal and Charismatic community. Their published research in *Global Pentecostalism: The New Face of Christian Social Engagement* showed that as much as 87 percent of religious-based international social relief is from the Pentecostal-Charismatic community.

As general superintendent of the Assemblies of God, I

have a unique perspective. I have the privileged opportunity to see churches across the US and throughout the world from a bird's-eye view. I see churches tearing down walls of racial division. I see churches distributing food to the hungry. I see churches rescuing girls from human traffickers. Above all of that I see churches sharing the life-changing hope of Jesus Christ with those who are lost and without hope.

I know that Choco's passion is to show Christ to the world through words and deeds. Although this book was written while he served as lead pastor of New Life Covenant Church in Chicago, I've gotten to know Choco closely through his current assignment as general treasurer of the Assemblies of God. He continues to be a soul winner, wanting to reach as many people as possible with the good news of Jesus.

May the Lord use *Love Them Anyway* to help you fall in love with the people at the place you are called to serve.

—Doug Clay
General Superintendent, Assemblies of God

INTRODUCTION

When I began to write the manuscript for this book, our country was suffering from racial division and political polarization. That was before the calendar turned to 2020. I had no idea a pandemic was right around the corner, no one could foresee the widespread protests over police shootings of black people, and I certainly didn't anticipate the rage over our presidential election!

Initially I wrote this book to address the emotional barriers and bitterness that had poisoned our discourse—inside and outside our church walls. And now the barriers are higher and the bitterness is deeper than I ever imagined.

People expect me, as a spiritual leader, to take sides on every issue in the news. Those who know me are well aware that I have very strong views on many different issues, but let me assure you from the outset that I'm not taking a hard-right or far-left stance on this problem or that one. I'm proposing a third way, the way of Jesus, one that values God's justice, kindness, and righteousness above every other point of view—it's the perspective and the lifestyle of the kingdom of God. His kingdom is upside down from the way the world operates. When Jesus' love and forgiveness fill our hearts and guide our steps, we'll listen more and we'll try to understand those who disagree with us without hedging our values. We'll be salt instead of sandpaper, and we'll be a source of light instead of letting our prejudices and political views become a dark cloud of resentment.

You may already be shaking your head and mumbling, "I knew it. He's a _____!" But I beg you, please don't write me off so quickly. Honor me by reading this book, and ask God to give you His wisdom as you read. Challenge me all you want, but please be open to the Spirit of God speaking grace and truth to your heart. And then obey Him by living in a way that reflects the gentleness and power of Jesus.

Today we're even more polarized than we were when I began writing this book. More than ever we need to experience God's kindness as we try to live according to His truth. That's the only way we'll have the motivation and the power to *love them anyway.*

CHAPTER 1

FENCES AND GATES

BEFORE MAY 25, 2020, black leaders could list dozens of incidents when the police killed black men—but this one was different. It must have been the fact that it was so visible and agonizingly slow and the response seemed so callous. The nation and the world watched as a Minneapolis police officer pressed his knee into George Floyd's neck for more than eight minutes. Protests started the next day, and they lasted for weeks, turning violent in some cities. I know something about the cause and the devastation of riots because I've experienced one.

Back in the early 1970s, when I was growing up in Humboldt Park, a Puerto Rican community in Chicago, fear and hate hung in the air. My neighborhood was labeled the worst in the nation, and deservedly so. Different gangs claimed each corner of the park and the streets beyond. One of my brothers led one of the gangs, so our family was deeply immersed in the atmosphere of crime, violence, fear, and hatred.

I was eight years old when my father abandoned our family

in 1972. My mom then had to look after her five sons and a daughter, including me, the youngest of the six. I struggled in school; I failed third grade because I couldn't read. With no father, no Jesus, and no future, it seemed that things couldn't get worse, but they did.

Five years later, just after the Puerto Rican Day Parade in Humboldt Park on June 4, 1977, gang warfare erupted between the Latin Kings and the Spanish Cobras. When the police arrived, they opened fire. At the time, the department was almost entirely white. A police sergeant killed two Latino men, and rumors circulated that they were shot in the back. Tension escalated. When police tried to close the park, they "were met with a barrage of bricks, bottles, stones, sticks and chairs. But Hispanic witnesses charged that policemen stormed the park with nightsticks and attacked many picnickers, including families with children,"[1] according to a local news report.

Immediately, violence broke out. The gangs—often at each other's throats—found a common enemy in the police, and resistance united them. Rioters threw Molotov cocktails, bottles, rocks, and anything else they could find. The hatred wasn't one-sided: some observed a Chicago cop lighting a Puerto Rican flag on fire, then waving it high in the air before dropping the flaming flag and stomping on it. Of the three thousand people involved in the riot, 116 were injured and 119 were arrested. In addition, thirty-eight police officers were hurt.[2]

The riots lasted a day and a half. Police cars were torched, and paddy wagons were overturned. When the police pushed people out of one part of the park, they gathered in another place with even more anger.

I was right in the middle of it all. This was our neighborhood, and these were our people. I was just a boy, thirteen at the time. Friends gave me the nickname "Choco"—because I loved chocolate so much—that has stuck to this day. But back then, I roamed the streets with everyone else. I remember wandering through the streets in disbelief as I watched the bloodshed and saw the rage in people's eyes. My big brothers were nearby, so I wasn't afraid. I knew they'd protect me.

During the riot, the streets were in chaos. Store owners locked their doors, but looters broke windows, climbed through the broken glass, and seized anything and everything they could. I watched people stream in and out of a small grocery store at the corner of Division and California Streets. They stole cases and armloads of things. What they were doing looked so normal that I stepped through the broken glass of the front door and walked over to the display cooler. I opened the refrigerator and took a bottle of soda—just one bottle—and closed the glass door. (I may have been a thief, but at least I closed the door just like my mom taught me.)

I had walked only a few steps down Division Street when I sensed a voice saying, "Put it back." At the time, I had no grasp of anything spiritual in my life, but later I understood that it was the Holy Spirit speaking to me.

I stood still on the sidewalk wondering what to do. Looters were chaotically running all around me with boxes of food and cases of drinks, but something propelled me to turn on my heels, walk back through the shattered front door of the store, dodge more people running in and out, and put the bottle of soda on the shelf, right where I found it. (And of course, I closed the refrigerator door before I walked out.)

At that moment, I wondered what was wrong with me. How could all these rioters feel happy and excited about stealing lots of stuff but I didn't feel good about taking one bottle of soda?

Back on Division Street the noise was deafening: sirens screamed, people yelled, and cars screeched their tires in a mad rush to get somewhere fast. But where could I go? I had no idea. I felt confused. This was my community. These were my people. We were all outraged at the injustice of the police action, but I couldn't make it all fit together.

On the third day, the police finally got control of the situation, and the riot subsided. When things had calmed down, I walked through the neighborhood. Smoke from burning cars and houses filled the air. I felt tremendous sadness and anger. None of this needed to happen. The scars from the fires and destruction took time to heal, but the resentment against the police lasted much longer.

One year later, the mayor offered to hire thousands of young people during the summer break to clean the streets of Chicago. The three-month program was the city's only specific response to the Humboldt Park riots and viewed as a way to give us something to do while we were out of school and make the city look nicer.

The mayor and a commission, who'd listened to the demands of the Puerto Rican community for summer employment, allocated $471,000 to fund these community service jobs.[3] The rules were that each person had to be at least fifteen years old. I was only fourteen at the time, but I applied anyway because I needed the money.

When I got my assignment, I was directed to meet with a supervisor and other kids at an Assembly of God church in our community. I thought I was going to be cleaning streets or a playground, but instead I was hired to help with their Vacation Bible School. (Believe me, I didn't know what I was getting into. I had no idea what VBS was!)

Day after day and week after week, when I arrived each morning, I saw young people praying and singing together. I saw a different countenance on their faces: instead of hatred, I saw love; instead of fear, I saw joy. I was fascinated. I'd never been around people like this, so I sat in the back and soaked it all in.

In August, I asked the supervisor to tell me more about what these kids were doing each morning. He smiled and said, "They're praying to Jesus."

He must have noticed that I was interested because he asked me, "Do you know Jesus?" I shrugged, so he asked another pertinent question: "Do you want to know Him?"

"Sure," I replied. I wanted what those kids had.

He called the other kids to come over. He told them I wanted to know Jesus, and he asked them to form a circle around me.

Well, that wasn't going to happen! A circle was gang language, not love language. Gangs put people in the middle of a circle as part of their initiation and then give them a beatdown. I didn't want that kind of initiation to Christ! They convinced me that no one was going to hit me, so I let them gather around me. They told me to close my eyes, but I wasn't going to do that. Then I heard them pray for me, prompting me to pray, "God, if You exist, change my life." I began attending that little church with the friends I'd met at VBS that summer.

A NEW DIRECTION

In November of that year, several of us went to a Christian convention. I'd never been to anything like that and didn't even know events like this even happened.

On the first night, the preacher told us about Jesus. When he called people to respond and come to the altar, I went forward. (Actually I went forward in every altar call during this period of my life because I wanted to make sure every door of my heart was open to Him.)

While I knelt at the front, a lady came over, laid her hands on me, prayed, and prophesied, "I've called you to be a great leader. Stay in My path. I will bless those who bless you, and I will curse those who curse you."

I was amazed and felt special in the eyes of God. I sensed that He had noticed me and was calling me to do something significant for Him. I felt like I had been given a new purpose and a new direction for my life. I had no idea what it might be, but this moment felt like a turning point. Up until then, my greatest hope was to play baseball in the major leagues, but now I realized God had something different for me.

As I walked back to the hotel, I thought long and hard about the prophetic word spoken over me and what it might mean. When I stepped into an elevator to go to my room, a tall Anglo man in a suit got on with me. As soon as the doors closed, he turned to me and said, "Have you not heard? I've called you to be a great leader. Stay in My path. I will bless those who bless you, and I will curse those who curse you."

Was I in the twilight zone? When the doors opened, I couldn't wait to get off the elevator. Walking down the hallway, I wondered what in the world this twice-spoken message meant. Who are these people? How did they get this message? How is this going to shape my life?

I didn't understand how the spiritual world operates, but I sensed these words were somehow God's message to me. I used them as fuel to give me energy, as stripes on the road to keep me out of the ditches. When I was a sophomore at Roberto Clemente High School in Humboldt Park, I was known as "the preacher kid" because I always carried my Bible with me. The high-rise school had eight floors and over five thousand students. I started a breakfast prayer club on the fourth floor. One day after the bell rang to change classes, I rode the escalator down to my next class. I looked down and saw four Hispanic kids beating a white student. That was not unusual: the school was predominantly Hispanic with some African Americans, but there were only a handful of white students. The way things worked out, almost every floor was ruled by a different gang. This white kid was in the wrong place at the wrong time.

I jumped over the side of the escalator and ran to the fight. I got in front of the white kid and told the Hispanic boys, "If you want to hit somebody, hit me!"

One of them smirked and waved me off. "This isn't your fight," he said. "Get out of the way."

I was defiant. "That's not going to happen! You're going to have to take me out if you want to get to him."

After a few tense seconds, the boys looked at each other, shrugged, and walked away. I turned around and helped the white kid stand up. He thanked me, and we both went to our next class. Turns out I never saw him again, but that wasn't the point.

The injustice I'd seen in the riots a few years earlier had

been repeated that day on the fourth-floor landing at the high school. I witnessed an innocent person being hurt, but this time, I had the opportunity to do something about it. I couldn't just walk past the boy being beaten up. I had to get involved. I had to be a leader and defend the defenseless. I'd been reading in the Bible about Jesus stepping in to care for people in trouble, and although I didn't understand it all, I had a strong feeling that He wanted me to follow His example to love, protect, and defend people.

Even though I was aware that fear and hate were all around me, I couldn't give in to those powerful emotions. I wanted to live in the reality of Jesus' presence and purpose. Because God was working in my heart, I knew God wanted me to love those being brutalized by others. But I also saw the people who were the persecutors and perpetrators, and I knew God wanted me to love them too. That's when I first began to understand that no one was off-limits to the love of Jesus.

The accounts in the Gospels of Jesus stepping into the lives of hurting people weren't just interesting anecdotes to me—they were more than that. Those scriptural accounts let me look into the compassionate heart of God. In Jesus, love wasn't just an idea or a philosophy; it was an expression of His character. Jesus was as bold as a lion and as gentle as a lamb. That's what it takes to love like He loves. When He saw people in trouble, He acted. He brought healing to the sick, forgiveness to the wayward, power to the powerless, and light to those in darkness. That's the kind of person He was calling me to be, and that's the kind of person He's calling you to be.

The problem, of course, is that being the person Jesus is

calling you to be is both the greatest adventure and the biggest challenge life has to offer. If you're finding that difficult, then you're not the first person to come to that conclusion.

FAMOUS AND INFAMOUS

If you were to ask people to name Jesus' most memorable parable (an earthly story with a heavenly meaning), most people would put the parable of the prodigal son at the top of the list. And rightly so. The story may be very familiar, but many miss the main point. This section of Scripture actually has three stories, and they're all about something that was lost: a lost sheep, a lost coin, and a lost son (or actually two lost sons). Luke starts us off by painting this picture: "Now the tax collectors and sinners were all gathering around to hear Jesus. But the Pharisees and the teachers of the law muttered, 'This man welcomes sinners and eats with them'" (Luke 15:1–2).

This scene was as emotionally tense as Humboldt Park was during the riots. Two sides didn't trust each other, didn't like each other, and didn't want anything to do with each other. Back then, the tax collectors didn't have respectable jobs like IRS employees have today. These were Jews who collaborated with the Roman occupying force to extract taxes from their countrymen. Tax collectors were considered traitors, and the people despised them.

What about the sinners who were mentioned? Sinners were a class of people that included prostitutes and thieves. Quite frankly, they were the scum of the earth. What were they doing? They were hanging out with Jesus and eating with Him. In that culture, eating a meal with someone signified acceptance and welcome. The outcasts of society felt completely at home around Jesus, and that made the religious leaders furious!

During that time in Palestine, the Pharisees and the teachers of the law were the ones who upheld the traditions of the Jewish faith during the demoralizing occupation by the Roman legions. They were the custodians of God's truth, the scrolls of the Bible, and were diligent about protecting the faith from any threats—threats like traitorous tax collectors, blatant sinners, and anyone who stooped to get involved with them. Was Jesus a threat to the religious leaders? Absolutely! They believed His acceptance of outcasts and misfits was completely wrong, against God's law, and detrimental to God's purposes. That's why they muttered in disgust when they walked up to the scene.

In response to their contempt, Jesus told the three "lost" stories. In the first, a sheep was lost, and the shepherd left the ninety-nine others to look for it. I can almost see the look of joy on Jesus' face when He explained,

> And when he finds it, he joyfully puts it on his shoulders and goes home. Then he calls his friends and neighbors together and says, "Rejoice with me; I have found my lost sheep." I tell you that in the same way there will be more rejoicing in heaven over one sinner who repents than over ninety-nine righteous persons who do not need to repent.
>
> —LUKE 15:5–7

Then He told them about a woman who had ten silver coins, perhaps given to her by her father as her dowry,[4] making those coins her most precious possessions. When she lost one, she lit a lamp in the house that probably had no windows, swept the dirt floor to look in every corner, and scoured the room until she found it.

The smile came back to Jesus' face when He told both audiences around Him,

> And when she finds it, she calls her friends and neighbors together and says, "Rejoice with me; I have found my lost coin." In the same way, I tell you, there is rejoicing in the presence of the angels of God over one sinner who repents.
>
> —LUKE 15:9–10

The third story is longer and more complicated, plus there's a twist in the plot. In this parable a father has two sons. The younger brother has lived in the love and prosperity of the family, but in his selfishness, he asks his dad for his share of the inheritance so he can leave home and live as he pleases.

In that day, the older son got a double share of the inheritance, so in essence the younger son was asking for a third of the estate. They didn't have stocks and savings in those days. Wealth was in land and livestock. The father must have been brokenhearted, but he sold enough to give his son all that he asked for.

The boy left home and wasted his wealth on wine, women, and song. When he was dead broke, a famine devastated the land. In his poverty and hunger, the only job he could find was feeding a farmer's pigs. For a Jewish kid, this was the greatest indignity since pigs weren't even supposed to be touched, let alone eaten. Finally, "when he came to his senses" (v. 17), the younger boy started the long trek home. Since the most he could hope for was to become a hired hand on his father's estate, he practiced his apology on the way.

As the boy approached home, his dad saw him from a distance and hiked up his robes so he could run to his son. The boy probably wondered what kind of greeting this might be. When his father got to him, the old man hugged him and kissed him. When the boy started into his confession, his dad interrupted him.

> But the father said to his servants, "Quick! Bring the best robe and put it on him. Put a ring on his finger and sandals on his feet. Bring the fattened calf and kill it. Let's have a feast and celebrate. For this son of mine was dead and is alive again; he was lost and is found." So they began to celebrate.
>
> —LUKE 15:22–24

What a great story about a father's grace-filled love for his wayward son! But that's only half of Jesus' message. When the older brother heard the sound of a party, he discovered that his wayward brother had come home, and he was furious. When he refused to join the celebration, his dad went to him and begged him to come. Still, he refused. The elder son argued that he had been obedient while that "son of yours" wasted much of the estate (v. 30). He added that he had worked hard while his brother partied and blew all his money, and now his dad was throwing a lavish party with a fattened calf for dinner to boot! He'd never even gotten a goat to eat with his friends.

The older son felt angry and self-righteous at the same time. Even though he believed his anger at his brother and his father were completely justified, I've often wondered why the older brother was so furious. It occurred to me that someone had to pay for the robe, the ring, the sandals, and the banquet—and since he was the heir, all that money was coming out of his own pocket, maybe not at that moment but certainly later. That's why he was so angry.

In a moment of great tenderness, the father tells him:

> My son,...you are always with me, and everything I have is yours. But we had to celebrate and be glad, because this brother of yours was dead and is alive again; he was lost and is found.
>
> —Luke 15:31–32

So, to put this all together:

- The father represents God.

- The younger brother represents the tax collectors, prostitutes, pimps, and thieves.

- The older brother represents the religious leaders.

In the first two stories, someone looked for the sheep and the coin. Jesus said this is a picture of people who go out to find the lost and point them to God for salvation, and heaven rejoices when the lost are found. But in the third story, who went to look for the lost younger son? Nobody. Who should have looked for him? That's right—the elder brother.

Jesus broke social and religious boundaries to love those whom the religious people detested. He didn't just love them at arm's length—He ate with them, laughed with them, and made them feel completely comfortable. Jesus is the true elder brother who left His comfortable home in heaven to search for us, find us, and bring us home. And if you follow

Him, you'll become a true elder brother who loves sinners so much that they'll feel accepted and celebrated.

When Jesus got to the place in the story where the father was inviting his angry older son to come to the feast to celebrate his brother's return, the dad called him "my son," or "my child," a term of wonderful tenderness. Jesus wasn't blasting the Pharisees for not loving the people who were having dinner with Him. He was pleading with them—and us—to join Him in God's great purpose of seeking and saving the lost. The moment is even more moving because Jesus knew that these Pharisees would collaborate with the Romans to have Him crucified only a few months later. Just as He was gracious to outcasts, He was equally gracious to those who hated Him.

It's human nature to put others down and feel superior to them. We find flaws in others and resent them. But that's not the way of the cross. Yes, there are plenty of ways people offend us and plenty of reasons to stay away from them, but Jesus calls us to love them anyway. Jesus was criticized for loving too much. What would our world be like today if people criticized us for that "flaw" instead of our being angry, judgmental, and indifferent to other people's problems?

> Jesus broke social and religious boundaries to love those whom the religious people detested.

Being religious isn't love, and insisting that we're always right is repulsive. Jesus moved past those barriers to love the "younger brothers" by eating a meal with them and to love the "elder brothers" scowling at Him for accepting people who were far off track.

NO BARRIERS

The little church I started attending when I was a teen became my spiritual home. Throughout my teen years, I served in many different ways and grew in my faith. Humboldt Park remained a crime-infested neighborhood, however, and the church often experienced break-ins and vandalism. Thieves stole music equipment, and gang members threw rocks through windows. The church replaced the broken glass a few times, but eventually the elders decided to brick in the windows. The church already had a fence but erected a strong gate to keep people out and prevent theft. Looking back, I'd have to say that the gate was motivated by fear and self-protection, not love. The Pharisees missed the love of Jesus because they were afraid of losing their high position and the power that came with it. Are you and I any different?

You may be thinking, "What is Choco accusing me of? Where is he going with this? Does he assume I'm a Pharisee?"

These are very good questions. They're exactly the questions I hope you're asking. Now let me ask you a few direct questions:

- Think about the two groups of people around Jesus as He tells these three stories. Are you more like Him or more like the Pharisees?

- Do people who are far from God feel loved and comfortable in your presence?

- Do you go to places where they are so you can search for them and find them, or do you avoid those places and those people because you consider them unacceptable?

- Do people know that even if you don't agree
  with them politically or affirm their lifestyle
  that you still love them anyway?

To help you think through these questions, let me pry into your heart just a little more.

We can define and describe love in many different ways. For instance, British professor and Christian philosopher C. S. Lewis identified four loves.[5] For our purposes, I want to focus on two types of love: because-of love and in-spite-of love.

The vast majority of the love we experience is conditional. We love somebody because the person has some admirable traits, makes us feel good, or enhances our reputation in some way. I'm not sure I've ever heard a popular song about love that wasn't about this kind of affection or fondness. This type of love is attractive and even intoxicating because no matter how much love you get, you're always afraid it won't last or be enough.

The other kind of love is the exact opposite. We love somebody in spite of his or her flaws, in spite of how that person makes us feel. You love even when your relationship with that person causes others to question your sanity and even tarnish your reputation. That's the kind of love Jesus had (and has) both for those who are blatant sinners and for the better-than-you, nose-in-the-air church people.

Because-of love produces comparison, worry, and fear because this type of love can easily be lost. But in-spite-of love isn't shaken by disagreements, flaws, and struggles. This is the sacrificial love that puts a lump in your throat when you hear about soldiers who suffer and die for each other. This is the it's-about-you-and-not-about-me kind of love when you take time to listen to people who hold convictions and practice lifestyles that are different from yours.

This kind of love is stunning because it's seldom seen these days, but when it's real, it's contagious. In-spite-of love breaks through defenses and destroys walls that divide us. It's costly. It requires time and humility. At least for a while, it's very uncomfortable, but it's worth it. Genuine love pulls you toward people you used to avoid, and it pushes you beyond your previous boundaries. Love like this asks more from you than you've ever given. It's inconvenient, and it's not safe.

In-spite-of love is beautiful, and it changes lives—yours and others'. All of us have individuals and classes of people we may tolerate but we don't truly love. If we're honest, we may have to admit we genuinely despise certain people. Love is the answer, but only if we admit our resistance, fill the holes in our hearts with God's in-spite-of love, and choose to love them anyway.

Jesus asks you to see people and situations through His lens of faith, hope, and love. When you do that, your passions will be redirected, your purpose will be refined, and you'll see God use you in ways you never imagined.

Choosing to love has always been one of the most important challenges for God's people. It's easy to see the world through the lens of what will give you the most pleasure, prestige, or power, but Jesus asks you to see people and situations through His lens of faith, hope, and love. When you do that, your passions will be redirected, your purpose will be refined, and you'll see God use you in ways you never imagined. Isn't that what you really want?

Now that we've come to the end of the first chapter, I've

prepared some questions to stimulate reflection and prayer and, hopefully, great discussions with your family, friends, and small group. Don't rush through these. You're not on the clock! Instead, take time to consider what God is saying to you as you and your group answer the questions.

DISCUSSION QUESTIONS

- Describe the environment of your childhood, family, neighborhood, opportunities, and hardships.

- How did these experiences shape your optimism or pessimism? Your faith or your doubts?

- Read the first two verses of Luke 15 again. If you had been a tax collector or a prostitute when you heard Jesus tell these three stories with the Pharisees standing next to you, how would you have felt? How would you have responded?

- If you'd been a Pharisee, someone learned and respected in your culture, how would you have felt and responded after Jesus told these three stories?

- As you think about the two groups of people around Jesus as He told these parables, have you acted more like Him or more like the Pharisees?

- Do people who are far from God feel loved and comfortable in your presence?

- Do you go to places where people you might not readily love hang out, or do you avoid those places because you consider them unacceptable?

ACTION POINT: WHAT LOVE LOOKS LIKE

A commitment to love like Jesus starts with a humble and honest analysis of the condition of our hearts. None of us love as deeply and compassionately as Jesus does, so we all have some steps to take. Identify the fences you've erected to protect yourself and keep people out. I'm sure those barriers seem reasonable, but do they keep you from connecting with and loving people Jesus wants you to love? This week, move toward one person each day whom you wouldn't normally engage. Speak a word of kindness, and see what happens.

CHAPTER 2

THE DIVIDE

THE LIFE-CHANGING—or should I say life-affirming— messages I received from the lady at the altar and the man in the elevator were obviously from God, and I knew it. From that moment, I believed God was calling me to make a difference as a leader.

In Humboldt Park, the damage inflicted by the injustice surrounding me was inescapable, glaring, and plain. I decided to do something about it by seeking a career in law enforcement. I zeroed in on becoming an Illinois state trooper, which seemed an unlikely choice to my friends because they knew about my employment history, starting with working several years in a jewelry store. Then, after I met the CEO of Chicago Public Schools at one of our church outreaches, he asked me to become his executive assistant. I found out I was good at follow-through and details, and the pay was really nice—$93,000 a year.

But in the back of my mind, I knew that becoming a trooper would put me in the middle of the injustice I was sure God wanted me to address. I firmly believed that a career in law enforcement would be the best way for me to have a positive impact on our community. I could protect the innocent and take criminals out of society. For me, being a Christian cop seemed like a perfect fit.

After eighteen months working in the Chicago public school system, I felt it was time to make the change. The process to become a trooper included the application and recruitment exam, a test of physical fitness, two interviews, psychological evaluations, and completion of training at the Illinois State Police Academy.

By this time, I had married Elizabeth Marrero, the daughter of the pastor of the church where I'd gone the summer when I was fourteen, where I'd trusted Jesus and begun to grow in my faith. As the day approached to take yet another exam, my father-in-law told me he planned to retire and asked me if I'd consider becoming the new pastor. Shepherding a flock was a role I had never contemplated for even one second.

For a number of reasons, going into the ministry didn't make sense. The church was small, but an associate pastor had served there for over twenty years; surely he was a better candidate than I was. And I was so close to becoming a state trooper. The trajectory of my life was set.

The other issue weighing on me, frankly, was that if I became the pastor, my salary would be cut to $35,000 a year. How could Elizabeth and I and our kids live on that? Those were very good reasons to say "Thanks but no thanks." No, it just wasn't going to work.

I didn't want to offend my father-in-law, however, so I came up with a plan to guarantee that I wouldn't be the next pastor: I was willing to let him put my name up for consideration, but I'd accept only if all sixty-eight members of the church voted for me.

There was no way that could happen. I was so confident in the outcome that I continued to move forward with the process of becoming a state trooper. A couple of weeks later, when the church held a meeting for the members to vote, to my utter shock, all sixty-eight people voted for me! In an instant, my vision of being a state trooper vanished and my income would be cut by almost two-thirds. Being called into ministry was something I didn't take lightly, and I clearly understood that God was leading me in this direction. It's just that I had been sure that the prophetic words given to me years earlier—"I've called you to be a great leader. Stay in My path."—were directing me to a career in law enforcement so I could stand against injustice. After the church vote, though, I slowly realized that my role as a pastor was another way to stand against injustice. I was being asked to become the pastor of a church where a riot had destroyed the community, where gangs ruled the streets and drugs ruined lives. I had grown up here. This was my community. The more I thought about the opportunity, the more confident I became that I could move outside the walls of the church to connect with people in the neighborhood. After much prayer and consideration, I accepted the Lord's call on my life and agreed to take on the role of pastor.

Early on, we made two important decisions. First, we changed the name of the church, which was called the Palestine Christian Temple of the Assemblies of God—a name that doesn't exactly roll off the tongue. Some people assumed, quite naturally, that we were a church for Palestinians. In fact the *Chicago Tribune* newspaper called our office every time there was conflict in the Middle East, seeking a quote or two regarding the latest crisis. My standard answer to reporters: "I don't really have an opinion. We're Puerto Ricans."

Since I wanted the church to reach out to the community with a new, inclusive message, we renamed our congregation the New Life Covenant Church and got to work.

The second decision we made was about the building. One day as I walked up to the church, I stared at the strong gate in front of the entrance. Instantly, I realized that this formidable gate was more than a physical barrier; it was also a spiritual and psychological roadblock that screamed "Stay away!" I remember telling some of our leaders, "This gate has got to go!"

An older member asked, "But what about the stealing? Aren't you afraid people will break in?"

"Security isn't our biggest priority; outreach is," I replied. "And that huge gate sends the wrong message to the people we want to reach with the gospel. It's time to move beyond fear and beyond convenience so everyone feels welcome here."

These two decisions changed the narrative of our church. We were no longer self-focused and fearful; we were committed to be open, loving, and welcoming. Before, we sent competing messages to the community. Our words were loving; but the name of the church was confusing, and the physical barrier spoke of anything but love. Now we were open for God's business, open to love the people He loves— all of them, not just some of them.

We weren't going to remain secluded in an armory; we had our arms open to hug those who'd never been to church and those who'd been coming for years, the down-and-out and the up-and-coming, those who had no resources and those who had more than enough. No matter what they'd done, they could find forgiveness. No matter how devastated they were, they could find healing and hope. They could be from the Humboldt 'hood—black, white, Asian, or any other background—and be welcomed. No one was off-limits to God's love. No divide, no separation, no suspicion.

And that's how we got started at New Life Covenant Church.

INSULATED AND OUTRAGED

Jesus was incredibly approachable, vulnerable, and appealing, but today, the mood of many Christians is shaped more by the media than by the heart of God. Virtually every news program, newspaper, and social media outlet shows vicious, bitter divisions. Fear and anger get people's attention, and advertisers value attention above all else.

The digital world has revolutionized news coverage. A century ago, national mass-media networks of newspapers and radio, and later television, were committed to fact-based coverage. In recent years, people increasingly have gotten their "news" from social media, especially Facebook. But social media isn't designed to communicate hard facts; its goal is to grab attention for advertisers, and it seems nothing sells like fear and anger. Social media companies use sophisticated algorithms like News Feed Editor to track every click, predicting what people will "like" and providing videos and links that promise to keep them engaged.

In an article about this online wave of anger, Tobias Rose-Stockwell explains, "By traditional journalistic standards, however, the News Feed Editor is a very, very bad editor. It doesn't differentiate between factual information and things that merely look like facts (as we saw with the massive explosion of viral hoaxes during the 2016 election). It doesn't identify content that is profoundly biased, or stories that are designed to propagate fear, mistrust, or outrage."[1] The goal of these news feeds, Rose-Stockwell contends, isn't to communicate facts in a dispassionate way. Instead, it's to use dramatic, outrageous headlines to grab attention for advertisers, which then generates profits for the social media companies. That's why they call these stories "clickbait."

In this environment of fierce opposition, it's much easier to label people as "them" and conclude that those who disagree with us are stupid or foolish—or both. When this happens, they don't just have different positions based on their perspectives and reasons; we believe they're enemies who threaten our values and our way of life! Far more often, we're less dramatic in our compulsion to isolate ourselves from people we consider undesirable. We don't openly attack them, but we keep our distance and find ways to keep from engaging in any meaningful way.

It goes like this: We insulate ourselves for *protection* from crime, gangs, and drugs. We insulate ourselves for *comfort* to be with people who look like us, talk like us, believe like us, and eat the foods we like. And we insulate ourselves for *convenience* to be close to shopping, work, and good schools. It's completely reasonable... and it's terribly narrow.

Over the course of several summers, University of California, Berkeley sociologist Arlie Russell Hochschild studied people in Louisiana to discover why so many white, middle-class people felt overlooked and bypassed by others. In her book *Strangers in Their Own Land*, she reports that both conservatives and liberals have their own "deep stories"—narratives about who they are and what's valuable to them. These narratives don't have to actually *be* true, but they *feel* true.

Hochschild spent most of her time focusing on the conservatives, whose deep story is the classic American dream: if you work hard and play fair, you'll have a better life. The people she extensively interviewed were angry and disillusioned because they saw other people, especially blacks and Hispanics, "cutting in line" in front of them in the pursuit of the American dream. Others who presumably weren't working as hard and were getting special treatment were making more progress, and the middle-class white people concluded that just wasn't fair. This sense of injustice made them feel like victims, helpless to change the system. Hochschild explains the divide between conservative and liberal perspectives.

> Those on the far right I came to know felt two things. First, they felt the deep story was true. Second, they felt that liberals were saying it was not true, and that they themselves were *not feeling the right feelings*. Blacks and women who were beneficiaries of affirmative action, immigrants, refugees, and public employees were not *really* stealing their place in line, liberals said. *So don't feel resentful.* [President] Obama's help to these groups was not really a betrayal, liberals said. The success of those who cut ahead was not really at the expense of white men and their wives. In other words, the far right felt that the deep story was their *real* story and that there was a false PC [politically correct] cover-up *of* that story. They felt scorned. "People think we're not good people if we don't feel sorry for blacks and immigrants and Syrian refugees," one man

told me. "But I am a good person and I *don't* feel sorry for them."[2]

These conservative, white, middle-class men and women concluded they had become strangers in their own land, and they resented those who had gotten preferential treatment.

Many evangelical Christians share a similar story, and they add a sense of outrage that the tsunami of decisions by liberal courts and progressive laws passed by Congress and state legislatures is eroding their moral imperatives. In reaction, political populism combines with spiritual resentment, and the result is a siege mentality against the forces that oppose them.

I don't believe this is the attitude we should have. We should be known for our love, not our anger; for our compassion, not our fear. Love recognizes hard realities and chooses to move toward people with open hearts, open ears, and at least a temporarily closed mouth. We'll have plenty of time to express our thoughts but with more kindness and wisdom than if we speak too soon.

Let me be clear: I'm not saying we should accept things that bother us without speaking up. I'm not saying we should let others erode our values while we shrug our shoulders as if there's nothing we can do. What I'm saying is that Jesus didn't hate people who disagreed with Him. He spoke the truth to them, was incredibly patient with them, and sacrificed His life for them. Even though they opposed Him, He loved them anyway.

> We should be known for our love, not our anger; for our compassion, not our fear.

In 2012 I accompanied Pastor Rick Warren (author of the

mega-selling *The Purpose Driven Life*) and several other pastors to an HIV/AIDS conference in Washington, DC. About twenty-five thousand people attended, including doctors and nurses, social workers, community activists, and many from the LGBTQ community. In the foyer, vendors were selling condoms that glowed in the dark, inflatable genitalia, and all sorts of things I won't mention.

We felt completely out of place. Talk about strangers in our own land! A gay man from Chicago heard I was at the conference. He tracked me down to invite me to lunch. As soon as we sat down, he looked at me with a sense of astonishment and asked, "Pastor, what in the world are you doing here?"

"I just want to be like Jesus and go to where the people are," I replied. "I'm here to love you."

He looked confused, so I continued to explain myself. "Look, your lifestyle doesn't frighten me. We don't have to agree for me to love you, and you don't have to change for me to love you."

We talked for two hours, and we parted as friends who understood each other better than before. Today, I see him occasionally, and I'm glad to connect each time. He invariably gives me a big hug because we have a bond based on unconditional love. Don't misunderstand: he knows I don't support gay activism, but he also knows I care about him even if he never changes his lifestyle or his convictions.

The news media—on both sides of the political spectrum—wants to inflame people to get attention and sell ads, so they use rhetoric that creates fear and outrage. Christians have jumped in with both feet and often defend their ground like the gangs on the corners at Humboldt Park. They express their intense feelings about immigration, guns, health care, taxes, and every other issue. They grab their corner to defend, but they should be grabbing the cross and representing Jesus.

In defense of Christian values, some of us use unchristian methods and words. Jesus was amazingly patient with clueless and impulsive disciples, and if we learn to love like Him, we'll be patient enough to be a bridge between competing factions. Our demeanor should welcome interaction, understanding, and trust so we can find workable solutions to seemingly intractable problems.

A 2017 study by the Pew Research Center reports that the partisan political divide over racial discrimination, immigration, welfare for the needy, and international diplomacy has risen rapidly in the past twenty-five years. The ideological gap is much larger than differences in age, gender, race, education, or church attendance.[3] The common term used to describe this polarization is *tribalism,* meaning we're intensely loyal to our tribe that believes and votes like us.

Other studies show that the differences aren't primarily conceptual; they're driven by powerful emotions, using an array of negative stereotypes and labels (hypocrites, selfish, cruel, stupid, etc.) to demean the other side.[4] Sadly—and, from my point of view, alarmingly—many Christians, including Christian leaders, voice these condemning, passionately held views. They feel completely justified in their fury, which makes them determined to dominate and defeat people who disagree with them instead of listening, having meaningful conversations, finding common ground, and building true friendships. We won't be able to bridge the divide if we stand back and condemn or if we leave.

As our three children were growing up, Elizabeth and I realized we needed a bigger house, and we wanted our kids to attend the best schools. The suburbs looked attractive—a bigger house for less money, far less crime, less noise, better schools, more convenient shopping, great restaurants—a move to the burbs sounded perfect.

But one night, I realized the convenience wasn't worth the price. I couldn't tell others to love like Jesus if we moved out of the neighborhood. Jesus lived among the people and gave Himself for others instead of looking for a place where He'd be more comfortable.

I told Elizabeth about my convictions, and she agreed. We bought a lot in Humboldt Park and built a house there. We wanted everyone to know that we were committed to the people in our neighborhood. Building a house anchored our family in the community. We wanted to face the same challenges everyone else faced, show up at the same events, enjoy the same relationships, fight the same fights for justice, and set down roots instead of being occasional visitors from outside the community. When others heard gunshots, we heard them too. When others faced discrimination, we stood shoulder to shoulder with them. When others feared gang violence, we understood the depth of their anxiety. When others celebrated births, anniversaries, and graduations, we were there to rejoice with them.

Elizabeth and I weren't going to run to the safety of the suburbs. Instead, we wanted to show that people can trust God in Humboldt Park and thrive as well by loving God, loving strangers, loving each other, and loving life.

HEART TRANSPLANT

I've seen a lot of people give in to bitterness and divisions, take sides, and despise people on the other side. I've known a few people who saw the damage inflicted by fear and hate, and they tried to be kind. Their efforts were noble, but the effect seldom lasted very long. We need more than determination; we need a heart transplant.

The prophet Ezekiel wrote and spoke during a time of calamity in the history of Israel. The nation had been devastated by foreign armies, and people were deeply discouraged. Even then, God was at work to change the hearts of His people. The pagan nations would know God's greatness and goodness only when God's people loved Him with all their hearts and lived for Him in all they did. Through the prophet, God promised them this:

> For I will take you out of the nations; I will gather you from all the countries and bring you back into your own land. I will sprinkle clean water on you, and you will be clean; I will cleanse you from all your impurities and from all your idols. I will give you a new heart and put a new spirit in you; I will remove from you your heart of stone and give you a heart of flesh. And I will put my Spirit in you and move you to follow my decrees and be careful to keep my laws. Then you will live in the land I gave your ancestors; you will be my people, and I will be your God.
>
> —Ezekiel 36:24–28

What is the sign of someone who has been given a new heart and is empowered by the Holy Spirit? It's that he or she follows God's laws. What laws? To love God with all our hearts and our neighbors as ourselves. A heart of stone is hard, angry, and demanding, but a new heart is filled with God's compassion for every person we encounter—including those who struggle because they've encountered outside forces like floods, fires, or crime, as well as those whose problems are self-inflicted. Jesus didn't distinguish between the deserving and the undeserving. He loved the leper *and* the woman caught in adultery.

When your heart is filled with compassion, you will learn to love like Jesus loves. People will notice, and they'll marvel at the greatness of God. Today, far too many people see Christians as angry conservatives more interested in winning political arguments than loving people. But when God gives you a new heart, people will be amazed.

In every interaction you have, God's reputation is at stake, and your heart and actions display His character...or not. God spoke through the prophet:

> I will show the holiness of my great name, which has been profaned among the nations, the name you have profaned among them. Then the nations will know that I am the LORD, declares the Sovereign LORD, when I am proved holy through you before their eyes.
>
> —EZEKIEL 36:23

We sometimes have the wrong understanding of holiness. It's not rigid adherence to strict rules. It's far more than that! Holiness is the essence underlying all of God's characteristics; it makes each part of His nature perfect and immeasurable. His love, wisdom, power, presence, and judgment are far beyond anything we can imagine. Our harsh, condemning attitudes and language profane the name of God, but when

His people have new hearts, people get a glimpse of God's greatness and mercy.

When His people display hearts of stone, people can't see the true nature of God. Our tender hearts, our positive attitudes, our gracious behavior, our love, our fight for justice for the oppressed—these are the things that make people thirsty for the God we follow.

> When your heart is filled with compassion, you will learn to love like Jesus loves. People will notice, and they'll marvel at the greatness of God.

EVEN THEM?

The currency of the kingdom of God isn't prayer, Bible study, missions, or service; it's love. All the disciplines are means to put us in touch with the love of God so it overflows into the lives of those around us. Whom does God want us to love? *Everyone.* Our love should know no bounds.

In Jesus' most famous sermon, He corrected the teaching of the religious leaders about people who opposed them:

> You have heard that it was said, "Love your neighbor and hate your enemy." But I tell you, love your enemies and pray for those who persecute you, that you may be children of your Father in heaven. He causes his sun to rise on the evil and the good, and sends rain on the righteous and the unrighteous. If you love those who love you, what reward will you get? Are not even the tax collectors doing that? And if you greet only your own people, what are you doing more than others? Do not even pagans do that? Be perfect, therefore, as your heavenly Father is perfect.
>
> —MATTHEW 5:43–48

The Old Testament doesn't tell people to hate their enemies. In fact the second commandment tells us to love our neighbor as ourselves (Lev. 19:18). But in Jesus' day, the religious leaders added to the teaching of Scripture. That's why Jesus said, "You have heard that it was said" instead of "It is written."

Does that seem radical? Unwise? And maybe insane to love our enemies? We need to remember that we were once God's enemies (Rom. 5:10), but God loved us so much that He sent Jesus to die the death we deserved so we could receive the honor He deserved. That's the measure of His love!

> Far too many people see Christians as angry conservatives more interested in winning political arguments than loving people.

When we love like that, we're following the example of our Father in heaven. Jesus explained that God's love knows no limits. He loves the just and the unjust. He blesses those who love Him and those who ignore Him or despise Him.

The love we experience and extend to our enemies isn't remotely like the usual way people talk about love. Most people love only those who love them. What's radical about that? Nothing. Even pagans love that way. But we're supposed to love even those who annoy us, who ignore us, who ridicule us, and who wish to harm us.

Jesus ends this part of the message with the startling command, "Be perfect, therefore, as your heavenly Father is perfect." If we're remotely honest, we have to admit that we're far from perfect. So, what does He mean? Jesus is pointing us to the perfection of God and, especially, His perfect love for outsiders and misfits, for the arrogant and the pitiful. The only way we can love like that is to soak up so much of the love of God that when our sponge is squeezed, love comes out.

Emotional conflict is seen not only in relationships with people across the political and economic divide but also in the family of God. Far too often, Christians harbor resentment toward other Christians. Instead of forgiving and loving, we gossip, withdraw, or openly criticize others.

On the night Jesus was betrayed, He gave the disciples plenty of instructions. In the early chapters of John's Gospel, he mentions love only a few times, but the concept and the word inundate the last several chapters. A key scripture is when Jesus tells His disciples, "A new command I give you: Love one another. As I have loved you, so you must love one another. By this everyone will know that you are my disciples, if you love one another" (John 13:34–35).

Was loving other believers a new concept? No, but it was new to love them "as I have loved you." I'm sure the disciples gulped as they looked around at each other. Only hours before, they had argued about who would take the prime positions of power when Jesus was crowned king. They were jealous and competitive. Now, Jesus was telling them to pour out the same compassion, attention, and care on each other that He had lavished on them.

> The currency of the kingdom of God isn't prayer, Bible study, missions, or service; it's love. All the disciplines are means to put us in touch with the love of God so it overflows into the lives of those around us.

These days, He's telling us to love the people in our churches with that same lavish love—tenderly, strongly, actively, and sacrificially. And again, He reminds us that everybody is watching when He says, "By this everyone will know that you are my disciples, if you love one another." If you criticize, condemn, and nitpick believers around you, then everyone will know that you *aren't* one of His disciples.

Are you thinking of someone right now? Sure you are. (Perhaps you're hoping no one is thinking about you!) The 411 on Christians is that we're really no different from people outside the family of God. Most of us are just as self-absorbed, just as distracted, and just as fearful and angry as those who never come to church.

> Most people love only those who love them. What's radical about that? Nothing. Even pagans love that way.

We're not the salt of the earth that makes people thirsty for Jesus, and we're not the light of the world that reveals the wonder of God's love and forgiveness.

In the last book of the Bible, John gives us a revelation of what is to come. In the opening chapters, though, he has an immediate audience: the churches in Asia Minor. Through John's prophetic voice, God addresses each one as a father gives direction to a son or daughter. In writing to the church in Ephesus, He praises them for their hard work to defend the faith against false teachers and for enduring hardship for the sake of the gospel. Then He says, "Yet I hold this against you: You have forsaken the love you had at first. Consider how far you have fallen! Repent and do the things you did at first" (Rev. 2:4–5).

I'm afraid this rebuke is appropriate for many of us today: we've forsaken our love for God, and we're pursuing things that may be important but are secondary. Love is the currency of God's kingdom, as I said, but many of us are broke because we've pursued other treasures, like power, popularity, prestige, and pleasure.

The divide is very real in our culture today. But God's love is still here, under the surface, and it's the love that heals wounds, builds bridges, and connects hearts. Division has become so common that love can feel weird and wrong at times. Some say we are against this and opposed to that; they say we want to control people and dominate the country. They say we do a lot more judging than loving.

We haven't done a good job of representing the Father who blesses the just and the unjust, who loves every person, and who is amazingly patient with those who disagree with Him. We need to change the impression people have of Christians and our Christ. We can do better. We *must* do better.

> Division has become so common that love can feel weird and wrong.

And it begins with us admitting our part in creating and extending the divide.

Can you imagine what difference we'd make if we all left church on Sunday so full of Jesus that we radiate His love to everyone we meet at work, at school, over the backyard fence, on the field, and in the stores?

Try to imagine it, and then start with the one person you're responsible for: yourself.

DISCUSSION QUESTIONS

- How would you describe the various divisions in this country—politically, racially, economically, and culturally?

- How have you seen social media inflame passions instead of communicate facts in news releases? Relate a recent example.

- Read Matthew 5:43–48 again. What are the biggest barriers to loving your enemies or at least those who disagree with you? Do you even want to love them? Why or why not?

- What are some reasons why it's hard to love some people in the family of God?

- Have you been part of the problem in creating and extending the divisions in our culture, or do you view yourself as part of the solution? Explain your answer.

ACTION POINT: WHAT LOVE LOOKS LIKE

Each day this week, engage in a conversation with at least one person outside your comfort zone. Don't grill the person. Just ask a couple of open-ended questions or invite an opinion…and don't give yours! You might ask something like this:

- Why do you think there's so much anger these days?

- What's your opinion of Christians and their solutions to the nation's problems?

- How do you think Christians could represent Jesus better?

CHAPTER 3

EVERYONE HAS A "THEM"

HAVE I MADE you uncomfortable yet? I hope so. Love demands more of us than many of us want to give. I understand that, but I hope you'll keep reading.

So far, I've addressed the deep suspicions and divisions in our nation, and I've encouraged you to "love them anyway." But quite often "they/them" aren't bicoastal liberal elites or forgotten conservatives in flyover states. They're closer than you think—and more personal.

When I was young, my "them" were the Latin Kings and Spanish Cobras. My "them" were also those with power and influence who neglected to do anything for those who looked like me in our community. Then, after Elizabeth and I had our three children, my "them" was someone who lived under my own roof—my only son.

When our third child was born, we named him Wilfredo Jr., but almost immediately he picked up the nickname Papito. He was a happy child, good-natured and ready to laugh. He was the picture of a well-loved little boy. In grammar school, his teachers told us he was a delight to have in class. Elizabeth and I were so proud of him. He loved baseball, had lots of friends, and even got along well with his two sisters.

We enrolled Papito in a private Christian school so he would get the best education in a Christ-centered environment. When he was in the sixth grade, something changed. We got notes from his teachers

> Love demands more of us than many of us want to give.

saying that he was causing disruptions with his antics. I wasn't worried when I received the first one, but by the third or fourth, I knew something wasn't right. Then I got a call from the principal's administrative assistant asking me for an appointment with the principal. When I sat down with him, he told me Papito was jumping over pews during chapel!

Unfortunately, these problems were just the beginning. He was attracted to kids who were sneaking behind the teachers' backs, thought cursing was cool, watched R-rated movies, and were interested in girls. In the middle of Papito's seventh grade, Elizabeth and I felt we should move him from his friends at the Christian school (surely it was their fault, not his!) into a public school. Honestly, I don't even remember praying about this decision—we just got into fix-it mode.

When I dropped him off for his first day of eighth grade at the new school, he opened the car door and walked down the sidewalk. As I watched him, tears streamed down my face. I had tried to give him a positive, Christian environment at the private school, but it didn't work. Now he was walking into a place where he'd encounter all the temptations of the world. I don't cry very often, but I wept when

I saw Papito slipping away from us. Soon, calls from concerned teachers resumed.

By the time Papito got to high school, he had become a different person. Years before, he had been a conscientious student. But now he was failing classes, and worse, he didn't care that he was failing. The teachers, understandably, had had enough. He seemingly spent more time in the principal's office than in class. Elizabeth and I tried everything, from the promise of rewards to threats of severe consequences. Nothing worked. At home, he spoke rudely to Elizabeth, slammed doors when he didn't get his way, and withdrew from all of us.

As many other parents know, it's heartbreaking to see your child take steps in the wrong direction. I wasn't angry, but I was deeply disappointed. What could we do? He had so much potential, but he was wasting it all. We determined to love him no matter what dumb decisions he made and no matter how much his behavior stained our family's reputation.

His one saving grace was that he loved baseball. When our son was a freshman in high school, he wanted to go to a private school with a first-class baseball team, and he even made a PowerPoint presentation to convince us that enrolling him there would motivate him to turn his life around.

How could we say no to that? He transferred to the school, but he connected with new friends who weren't a good influence. The fathers of two of his new friends were drug dealers. Papito snuck out to wild house parties and got involved in alcohol, marijuana, and sex. The lure of sin was greater than the security of our home.

To encourage him—and get him out of town for a while—we paid for him to go to the Dominican Republic to a special baseball camp lasting six weeks. We didn't want the ball-playing trip to be too easy for him, so we had him stay at a boys' orphanage that our church sponsors. Our thinking was if he lived as they lived, then he would learn to appreciate his own life.

Not long after his arrival, though, he complained about the living conditions. We weren't surprised, but we prayed and he stayed. When Papito got back home, it looked as if the experience had a dramatic impact: physically, he had changed, losing some weight and looking healthy, but more importantly, he had a new confidence about him. But the change didn't last long once he returned to Chicago. After a little while, Papito reverted back to his old habits and attitudes. Soon it was obvious that he'd rather be anywhere in the world than with Elizabeth and me, and he didn't even enjoy being with his sisters.

One day I sensed the Holy Spirit telling me to look in his car. It didn't take long for me to find a bag of marijuana. I walked in the house and held up the baggie in front of him.

"Son, what's this?" I asked.

He tried to say it belonged to someone else, but I knew that wasn't true.

"Son," I told him, "do you think you're stronger than me? Do you think you can wear me out so I'll give up on you? Do you think you can push me away so I don't care about you anymore?"

I let those questions sink in for a few seconds, and then I continued, "Let me assure you that I'm not tired and I won't quit. You're not stronger than me. No matter what you do, I love you so much that I'm going to keep coming for you.

And let me also assure you that God isn't going to give up on you. You're cornered by our love."

Can I share a secret? I was tired—so tired that I wanted to give up on my son. But the way my Father in heaven loved me gave me hope. It was the only way I knew to love.

I wish I could say this was the turning point and things got much better, but they didn't. He kept hanging out with people who were going nowhere, and he kept smoking weed. One day when I could tell he was high, I took him by the shoulders and told him, "Son, nothing you can do will make me love you more or less. You can't control how much I love you, but you can control how much I'm pleased with you. Right now, I'm not that pleased, and you know it. But I will always love you."

By his junior year, Papito was smoking weed every day. Elizabeth and I took his car keys and his phone. From his reaction, you would have thought we were skilled at the art of torture! We had long talks about his future. Well, that's not exactly accurate. Elizabeth and I had long talks about his future with him in the room, but he just sat and sulked. We spoke words of love, we spoke words of hope in his future, and we administered consequences for his wayward behavior. Those were the ways to love someone like Papito. Elizabeth later said that Papito taught her to pray. We spent many hours pouring out our hearts to God to change the direction of his life, and we shed many tears.

During Papito's senior year, the principal had told him that if he had thirty demerits, he should worry about graduating. By April, he had 130! The principal warned him that if he got one more, he would be expelled. A couple of hours later, Papito skipped his chemistry class. That was it. The principal called us into a meeting so he could tell us that Papito wouldn't be allowed to walk at graduation because he had skipped so many classes.

Elizabeth and I envisioned all the other proud parents watching their sons and daughters walk across the stage, and our hearts broke because this was another sign that our dear son was throwing his life away. We assured him this wasn't the end. He must have realized the importance of the moment because he apologized at a school board meeting. The board agreed to let him serve an in-school suspension for the rest of the year and complete his classwork. They didn't let him go to prom or walk at graduation, but he earned his diploma. He missed the ceremony, but at least he had the paper to show he had made it out of high school.

Papito had a full scholarship to play baseball at a college in St. Louis. He went there for a few days to get acquainted and meet some of the players, and they smoked weed together. And then, out of nowhere, something changed. I don't know if a light switch was flipped, but Papito realized that if he was acting like this the first few days of college, then his life would be a train wreck after four years. He knew he needed to follow a different path.

Miracle of miracles, Papito told us that he wanted to enroll in the Master's Commission, a three-year Christian leadership training school in Atlanta. Elizabeth and I were equally stunned and thrilled. We knew he'd be surrounded by godly people who taught the truth of God's Word to young men and women who were eager to serve Jesus with all their hearts.

Even there, Papito hadn't finished all his rebellious ways, but at least he was in an environment where people loved him and encouraged him to follow Jesus. Still, he drifted so much that he was asked to leave the Master's Commission after the second year. When he called to give me this news, I wondered if anything could make a dent in his heart. In Atlanta later that day, his girlfriend, Eden, wept as she recounted how he had messed up his life. Her tears had a powerful impact on him. He realized his choices had hurt someone he loved very deeply.

He came back to Chicago, and for the next two weeks, he basically laid in bed. He felt guilty, ashamed, and hopeless. One day Elizabeth walked in and saw him with the covers drawn over his head. She pulled the covers back and asked him, "When are you going to grow up?" In addition to his girlfriend, Elizabeth loved him enough to speak the truth to him. Her tone was strong, her words were true, and they pierced him like a spear. He realized he had been acting like a spoiled little boy, and it was time to become a man.

He transferred to Southeastern University in Lakeland, Florida, where he strengthened his relationship with Eden and got involved as a youth pastor in a local church, which was a strong sign that he was making a U-turn in his life. This time, his turnaround stuck.

Today, Papito and Eden are happily married, and he serves as the youth pastor at one of our campuses. We're so proud of him, and we're incredibly thankful to God that He turned our son around. There are no guarantees that if we love people far from God, they'll come back and follow Him, but our persistent, tenacious love is the best chance they've got.

During those hard years, my emotions were on a roller coaster of fear, discouragement, and confusion. No one in our family smoked marijuana or drank alcohol, though at one time my father had been an alcoholic, so we knew better than to mess with it. Hadn't I given Papito everything he could possibly want or need to be successful? I had paid for him to be in a Christian school, bought him expensive baseball equipment, and even hired a New York Yankees pitcher to give him lessons. Elizabeth and I had prayed for him every day, and we had tried to provide a loving, stable home.

In spite of those painful and powerful emotions, I determined to roll up my sleeves and love him through it all. No matter how he responded, I wasn't going to stop loving him, speaking the truth to him, saying it with kindness and firmness, and letting him suffer the consequences of his bad choices. That's the only way some people learn, and I wasn't going to short-circuit the painful but necessary process.

> There are no guarantees that if we love people far from God, they'll come back and follow Him, but our persistent, tenacious love is the best chance they've got.

I had to make the decision to love Papito every day—and actually many times each day. I often stood by his room when he was sleeping and pleaded with God to give me wisdom and power to love him. Day after day, I claimed the blood of Jesus over the dark powers that had him in their grip. This wasn't "now I lay me down to sleep" prayer; it was warfare against the evil forces in the universe!

During the hard years, Elizabeth fasted and prayed for Papito every Tuesday. For all those years, from seventh grade through high school and then to the Master's Commission, the tension was evident in my heart and in my prayers. There were a few brief periods when he seemed to turn a corner, but

I always had the nagging fear that it wouldn't last. Actually I never had a day off from my tenacious love for Papito because I never had a day off from my concern for him.

My own experience of God's unconditional love gave me the courage to wade in, and keep wading in, to my son's life—even when he wasn't responsive and even when he wished I'd just leave him alone. I didn't smother him, but I also didn't let him wonder if I was present. I wanted him to smell my cologne, to hear my voice, to feel my footsteps—not to intimidate him but to remind him that I love him.

CLOSE TO HOME

Our family's saga has a happy ending, but we're far from the only one that struggles with severe relational and emotional turmoil. The statistics are alarming:

- 20.3 million American adults battle with substance abuse.[1]

- 5.2 percent of girls meet the clinical criteria for eating disorders: anorexia, bulimia, or binge eating.[2]

- Anxiety disorders affect 40 million adults in America, or 18.1 percent of the population.[3]

- About 17.3 million adults in America had at least one major depressive episode in a recent year, which is 7.1 percent of the population.[4]

- More than 35 percent of women and 29 percent of men have experienced rape, physical violence, and/or stalking by a partner.[5]

- 40–50 percent of first marriages end in divorce, and the number is higher for subsequent marriages.[6]

This is just a sample of the many types of relational struggles, addictions, and mental illnesses that people battle every day, and they affect everyone in the family, not just the individual. In fact the ripple effects have consequences as the children grow up and have families of their own.

Beyond the sterile statistics, these are real people with complex and deep problems. Far too often, we don't want to step into the chaos and powerful emotions in our families, so we either ignore them or give simplistic answers to life's most daunting questions. Neither of these responses is propelled by love.

If your family doesn't struggle with these problems, it's easy to sit back and judge others, thinking, "At least I'm not like him...or her...or them." The rich assume the poor are irresponsible, and the poor sneer at the rich for being so selfish. Gays feel attacked by those who are straight, and straight people are afraid the LGBTQ community is eroding the nation's values. Immigrants wonder if they'll be accepted, and citizens believe their resources are being wasted on people who are here illegally. People in the cities look down at the rural communities and assume they're backward, and the country people can't imagine living in crowded, fast-paced, multicultural urban settings. The young assume that people over forty are dinosaurs, and those who are nearing retirement look at the millennials and mosaics and wonder what will happen to America. Some families have to set rules about what's off the table for discussions at Thanksgiving and Christmas because fierce arguments ruin these gatherings.

There has to be a better way.

Miroslav Volf lived through the horrors of the Yugoslav Wars in his native Croatia, and his brother was killed in the struggle. When he writes about forgiveness and reconciliation, he has immense credibility. In his book *Exclusion and Embrace*, he says this: "Forgiveness flounders because I exclude the enemy from the community of humans even as I exclude myself from the community of sinners."[7]

Isn't that the heart of the problem? Isn't that what we're doing when we make those who disagree with us into our enemies? Isn't that the reason we assume people are fools or stupid or evil if they have a different solution to the problems we see? We've caricatured them so we can write them off instead of seeing them as people created in the image of God with immeasurable worth.

Volf knows that hatred is normal but love is supernatural. Loving our enemies—that is, those we believe are our enemies—requires a genuine, life-changing experience of God's grace demonstrated on Calvary's hill. He explains in this manner.

> But no one can be in the presence of the God of the crucified Messiah for long without overcoming this double exclusion—without transposing the enemy from the sphere of the monstrous…into the sphere of shared humanity and himself or herself from the sphere of proud innocence into the sphere of common sinfulness.[8]

When we grasp the wonder of God's grace, we'll realize that evil won't last forever. When that happens, we'll have the security to be honest about our own sinfulness that required the Son of God to step out of the glory of heaven to die a shameful death in our place. And then we'll realize the ground is level at the foot of the cross, as the saying goes. Everyone is a sinner, everyone needs the cross, and God considers everyone so valuable that

> Hatred is normal, but love is supernatural.

He paid the ultimate price—for us and for those we used to consider "them."

When we rediscover our own sinfulness, we won't be so quick to condemn and exclude others. We'll realize how much we need mercy and understanding, which God has poured out on us in abundance through the cross, and we'll be quick to extend mercy and understanding to others. Again, this doesn't mean that we give up our values and views, but it means we give up our desire to obliterate or run away from those who don't hold the same values and views.

By the grace of God, "they" become "us" because we share a common humanity, common fallenness, and a common need for a Savior.

GAS ON THE FIRE

One of the biggest reasons people continue to be "them" is that we listen only to people who reinforce what we already believe. This is called confirmation bias. We engage in a conversation or turn on a news broadcast with a predetermined perspective. If people agree with us, we believe they're smart and wise and noble. If they disagree, we quickly conclude they're uninformed or foolish. Of course, this bias eliminates the give and take of healthy thinking and meaningful dialogue. We live in an echo chamber of voices that feel familiar and reinforce what we already believe. In an article for *Psychology Today*, Shahram Heshmat, PhD, explains:

> When people would like a certain idea or concept to be true, they end up believing it to be true. They are motivated by wishful thinking. This error leads the individual to stop gathering information when the evidence gathered so far confirms the views or prejudices one would like to be true.
>
> Once we have formed a view, we embrace information that confirms that view while ignoring, or rejecting, information that casts doubt on it. Confirmation bias suggests that we don't perceive circumstances objectively. We pick out those bits of data that make us feel good because they confirm our prejudices. Thus, we may become prisoners of our assumptions.[9]

When I think of confirmation bias, I think of the television show *Cheers*. Norm always walked in and spoke to the same people in the same way, sat in the same seat, and asked for the same drink, day after day. The routine felt familiar, and he didn't have to wrestle with competing ideas or desires. But his life was immensely predictable and boring.

> The ground is level at the foot of the cross....God considers everyone so valuable that He paid the ultimate price—for us and for those we used to consider "them."

Healthy disagreements are the spice of strong relationships. Sadly, many of us don't want to have them. We sit in the same seats at church, have the same friends, tell the same stories, and hold the same perspectives we've had for decades. It's a culture shock—an uncomfortable culture shock—to even think of spending time getting to know undocumented people, befriending someone in the LGBTQ community, listening to the other side talk about gun control, and sacrificing our time and resources for people who are very much unlike us.

When we're secure in our relationship with Christ, we can patiently listen to people who have differing opinions and lifestyles. We can be open to competing ideas and even utter the words we seldom hear today—"I don't know"—without feeling ashamed or belittled. In fact we will make a point of reading and listening to people who hold views that are different from ours so our thinking becomes deeper and we learn to appreciate the complexity of many issues we face. When we avoid confirmation bias, we can stop labeling people and disregarding them. And when we value them, we'll love them.

HOW CAN YOU TELL?

What are some of the signs that we've relegated individuals or segments of society to the status of "them"? I believe we can see observable, empirical evidence as well as emotional evidence. The empirical evidence appears when we objectively look at who our friends are, where we shop, where we live, and the way we talk about groups of people. Who is inside our circle? Who is conspicuously absent? If everyone in the circle is the same color as us, we probably have classified other races as "them."

> When we avoid confirmation bias, we can stop labeling people and disregarding them. And when we value them, we'll love them.

The emotional evidence may be even clearer. When you

see images of certain kinds of people (distinguished by their color, sexual preference, politics, gender, age, or nationality), does a feeling of disgust arise in you? Contempt is a powerful signal that you may consider those people "them."

Our churches are often segregated. Martin Luther King Jr. famously said that the hour of worship on Sunday morning is the most segregated hour in the week. We let the Hispanics reach Hispanics, blacks reach blacks, and whites reach whites. This isn't at all what the apostle Paul meant when he described

> Contempt is a powerful signal that you may consider those people "them."

the body of Christ, which is characterized by diversity. The gospel isn't the property of one ethnicity or race or color. Jesus died for us all, and He loves us all the same.

There are billions of people on the planet who aren't like you. They don't look like you, they don't dress like you, they don't talk like you, they don't believe like you, and they don't live like you. Does that make them inferior? Of course not. They are God's treasures just as you are. One of the ways we know we're getting in touch with the heart of God is when our circle of "us" expands and our circle of "them" shrinks.

Are you feeling uncomfortable now? I understand you might be, but all of us need God to stretch our horizons so we can have a bigger impact for the gospel. I think it's perfectly reasonable to assume that we won't have much of an impact on any people who are in our category of "them." When they know we don't value them and still talk to them about Jesus, they feel like targets instead of people we love.

Some of you are thinking, "Choco, this is none of your business! Who are you to tell me to reach out to people I don't like and who don't like me, who have a lifestyle I find abhorrent, who kill babies, who are irresponsible and a drain on our country, who are takers and have nothing to offer?"

Yes, I know that's what some of you are thinking. That's great. It shows you're paying attention. Keep reading. I'm afraid many of us have misplaced loves. We love our cat or dog, we love our baseball team, we love our favorite designer, but we don't love the people Jesus loved so much He died for them. Don't be surprised if you realize

> We won't have much of an impact on any people who are in our category of "them." When they know we don't value them and still talk to them about Jesus, they feel like targets instead of people we love.

that your love is narrow. The disciples' circle was too small, and the first-century Christians had circles that were too small. (See Paul's letter to the Galatians.) Throughout history, virtually everyone has been too stingy with his or her love. It's human nature, but it's not the nature of God.

You might want to ask me, "Choco, are you questioning whether I'm even a Christian?" The Bible says we'll know them by their fruit, and if the preeminent evidence of a connection with God is love for people who don't love us, some of you might wonder if your lack of love is really a lack of experience of God's grace. I'm not questioning your eternity, but I'm questioning the depth of your grasp of God's magnificent love.

These aren't theoretical, abstract issues. These questions are inherent in some of the most difficult questions we face in relationships. A woman in our church—I'll call her Felicia—has a daughter, Jessica, who is a lesbian. One time her daughter asked her if she was going to come to her wedding. Felicia came to me and asked what she should do. She was afraid that if she went, she would validate Jessica's lifestyle choice, but if she didn't, she would drive a wedge between her and her daughter. The wedding was almost a year away, so I told her, "Let's pray for wisdom. God will give it to you."

Months passed by. A few weeks before the wedding, I saw Felicia at church, and she asked, "Pastor, I've been praying. What do you think I should do?"

I answered, "I think you should go to the wedding. Jessica already knows you don't endorse her lifestyle, but being present shows her that nothing can stop you from loving her. That's important—now and for the rest of your life in your relationship with her. When you're there, God is present there in you, and Jessica needs to experience the presence and love of God." Now, I don't usually recommend Christians attend gay weddings because it does seem to convey an endorsement. In this instance I felt it was necessary for this mother to show this type of unconditional love to her daughter.

I saw Felicia again after the wedding, and she told me she had had a wonderful time with Jessica. I said, "Because you were there, you've left the door open with your daughter. If you hadn't gone, the door probably would be shut. Jesus opened doors with people who lived in ways that weren't God's design. You've followed His example. You now have the opportunity to share the love of Christ with Jessica in the future. You showed up. Love showed up."

There are two categories of "them": safe and unsafe. The safe ones are those that we can love without risk. They aren't going to oppose us, and they don't fight back. We can give clothes to Goodwill, canned goods to the food pantry, and money to any number of organizations that work with the underprivileged. It feels good to contribute to these people from a distance.

On the other hand, the unsafe ones try to shame us or intimidate us. They see us as a threat even when we go to them with humility and kindness. They know we disagree with them about sexual preference, guns, the border, abortion, or some other hot topic, and their outrage overshadows our desire to build bridges with them. In 2020 reason and bridge building seemed to go out the window. Indignation over racial inequality was met with furious defensiveness. Screams over a "stolen election" told the other side that there was no hope for dialogue. Far too often Christians were right in the middle of the name-calling and hatred. At that point, many of us weren't even thinking about building bridges—we just wanted to be heard. Overwhelmed by the constant negative rhetoric, many Christians began to lash out in response.

When I took a stand against a proposed new high school geared toward gay students, some people sent hate mail to me at the church office, while others called the mayor's office to complain. A few people did interviews on the local news and condemned me for being antigay because I opposed the school. I wasn't, and I'm not hostile toward gay people. I love them because Jesus loves me. But I'm against creating a powerful academic environment that legitimizes that lifestyle. I see a big difference between people and institutions, but the protestors assumed that my opposition to the school necessarily meant that I opposed them personally.

STAYING THE COURSE IN HAITI

When a magnitude 7.0 earthquake devastated Haiti in 2010, some estimate that 250,000 people died, and many of the survivors were homeless. We took a team to Port-au-Prince as soon as we could get in. The look on the Haitians' faces was a level of desperation I've seldom seen. They didn't have water, food, or shelter. Many had lost family members, or maybe worse, they couldn't find their loved ones and wondered if their parents or spouses or kids were under the immense piles of rubble.

We had loaded supplies onto a bus at the airport. When we arrived in a devastated area, people ran to us and clamored for anything we had. It was a madhouse! One of the men on our bus was so frightened that he told me, "Choco, let's give all this food to the army and let them give it out. And then let's get on the next flight out of here!"

I looked into his eyes and shook my head. "No, we're not going to do that," I said firmly. "We didn't come here for a vacation. Before I left home, I said goodbye to my wife and family. We're staying."

We settled in for a few days, providing supplies, but we also set up a medical clinic with triage to treat the wounds caused when masonry and steel crushed arms and legs. The entire time we were there, the Haitian people were so desperate for any assistance that they rushed trucks and grabbed anything they could put their hands on. It was uncomfortable and chaotic, but it was important for us to be the hands and feet of Jesus to them.

Back home, unsafe people may be a motorcycle gang, pimps and prostitutes, a gay couple, or a pedophile. The safe people may be a Middle Eastern couple who moved into the neighborhood, an undocumented family, or simply people from "the other side of town." Loving them doesn't mean we choose only to avoid throwing rocks at them; it means moving toward them, getting to know them, and loving them even when we see a dark side of their lives.

I'm sorry to say that for many of us, the unsafe "them" include the people in our churches, our Bible studies, and our families when we reach out to care for people outside our previous circle. When we choose to love, to sacrifice, to give to people others consider "them," we may take friendly fire; we may become "them" to the people who previously were comfortable with us.

EVERY REASON TO HATE

Let me tell you about a group of believers. They saw that their culture was crumbling around them. Unbelievers were taking their rights away, and they were angry. They gathered together to complain about their conditions, but they felt demoralized and worried about the future. They wanted to fight back but also wanted God to provide a quick solution to their problems. They believed they had a right for God to come through for them—and soon!

No, I'm not talking about modern America. I'm referring to the conquered Jews living in Babylon in the sixth century before Christ. Jerusalem had been destroyed by the Babylonian army, and many of the people had been led into exile. The Babylonians were powerful and brutal, and God's people were angry and confused.

How could God let this happen? Where was He? When was He going to make all this right? In the middle of their complaints, some of their prophets showed up and promised that God was going to get them out of there in a very short time, only two years, so they didn't have to figure out how to live as exiles.

But those prophets weren't speaking for God. Only the prophet Jeremiah was. God gave him a message to refute the false prophets: "Do not let the prophets and diviners among you deceive you. Do not listen to the dreams you encourage them to have. They are prophesying lies to you in my name. I have not sent them" (Jer. 29:8–9). And then He gave the people instructions that must have startled them:

> Build houses and settle down; plant gardens and eat what they produce. Marry and have sons and daughters; find wives for your sons and give your daughters in marriage, so that they too may have sons and daughters. Increase in number there; do not decrease. Also, seek the peace and prosperity of the city to which I have carried you into exile. Pray to the LORD for it, because if it prospers, you too will prosper.
>
> —JEREMIAH 29:5–7

God made several key points, the first being this: *don't expect to be out of here anytime soon.* If they had one foot out the door in Babylon, they wouldn't be involved in living to the fullest. Instead of hating the Babylonians and despising everything about them, God told them to "seek the peace and prosperity of the city" because "if it prospers, you too will prosper." God certainly didn't want His people to worship Babylonian gods, so they had to walk a line between engagement and separation. They had to be wise in their relationships, strong in their faith, persistent in their work, and hopeful that God would fulfill His promise.

I believe this is precisely God's word to us today. The Bible says we're exiles in a foreign land, but many Christians think and act like we're the bosses and the culture should bow to us. Only false prophets teach this misguided notion. The truth is that we're aliens, but even more, we're ambassadors who represent our King in a foreign land. To do our job well, we must speak the language of our new country but realize we're citizens of heaven. If we see ourselves as victims of our culture, our circle will be small, and we'll see a lot of people as unsafe "them."

How did the Jewish people get in this predicament? Certainly, the cruel Babylonians were responsible for destroying the nation and taking them into exile, but in God's directive to the people, He says that He carried them into exile.

At that point, they had a choice: they could look at their condition and complain that it wasn't fair and God had let them down, or they could realize that even in Babylon, God was with them and God had a sweeping purpose for them.

> If we see ourselves as victims of our culture, our circle will be small, and we'll see a lot of people as unsafe "them."

A few verses later, we find the promise many of us love to quote: "'For I know the plans I have for you,' declares the LORD, 'plans to prosper you and not to harm you, plans to give you hope and a future'" (Jer. 29:11). No matter how they arrived in Babylon, God wanted them to think and act like people who have a kingdom mindset and a kingdom determination. They couldn't be a light for the city unless they trusted God, engaged the foreign culture, stayed strong even as they loved people, and prayed for (instead of against) the people who had captured them.

This is a message we need to take to heart. Our commission is to seek the peace and prosperity of the city, nation, and culture where God has sent us. Elizabeth and I thought about moving out of Humboldt Park at one time, but we realized this was where God called us to thrive and where God called us to bless others.[10]

The principle applies to all of us, no matter where we live. We're here because God has put us in this place at this time in history. We can complain, isolate ourselves, and condemn others, or we can reach out and love the people around us. That's what Jesus did, and that's what God told His people to do when they were captives in Babylon. And that's what He's still telling His people to do.

DISCUSSION QUESTIONS

- Do you agree with the premise of this chapter that all of us have a "them"? Explain your answer.

- What is the empirical evidence that shows you who your "them" are?

- Who are the groups of people that automatically cause your blood pressure to rise and feelings of contempt to emerge—or at least a reluctance to associate with them? How long have you had these feelings? Where do you think they came from?

- Who are the safe "them" in your world? Who are the unsafe "them"?

- Read Jeremiah 29:5–7. What are the parallels between the exiles in Babylon and Christians today? How do God's instructions to them apply to us?

ACTION POINT: WHAT LOVE LOOKS LIKE

If you've identified at least one group of "them," take one step toward someone in this category each day this week.

If you haven't identified "them" in your life, ask your spouse or grown kids who they think your "them" are. And believe them. Then take a step toward "them" each day this week.

CHAPTER 4

TAKE THE BLINDERS OFF

I T WASN'T LIKE I was sitting around wondering how to fill my time. As a pastor I was incredibly busy. The church was growing, and I was pouring all my energies into leadership development, sermon preparation, long-range strategic planning, and managing people and resources to create effective programs. In addition, I had to deal with leaking pipes, holes in the roof, and other maintenance nightmares that always come with an old building.

In the winter blocks of ice formed on the gutters. We had to climb ladders and remove the ice so chunks didn't fall on people as they came to church. Every time we baptized people, the water in the baptismal tank leaked through the floor and flooded the restroom below. And every time that happened, we had to change the tile on the floor. Because there was so much to do, I was at the church ten to twelve hours a day, six days a week (and sometimes seven). I wasn't looking for something else to do.

The police commander of the fourteenth district of Chicago was a friend of mine. One day he came to my office. "Choco, we have a problem in Humboldt Park," he began. "Over the last nine months, we've arrested more than six hundred women for prostitution. This is an unprecedented number." He paused to let that fact sink in, and then he asked, "Is there anything you and your church can do to help us?"

I couldn't think of anything. Instantly I answered, "Yes, we'll pray for you." But inwardly I was thinking, "You've got problems, but I have problems too. I have leaks I can't seem to fix, young people who aren't ready to be leaders yet, and I have to preach every week." But of course, I didn't say those words. I thanked him for coming, and I again assured him we'd pray for him and his department. I could tell by his expression that this wasn't exactly the help he was looking for.

I went home that evening and told Elizabeth about my conversation with the commander, and then we went to bed. The next morning, I walked into the kitchen as she was making coffee. I told her, "Honey, last night God put it on my heart to buy a farm."

Elizabeth looked at me as if I'd said I'd seen an alien. "A farm? What do you know about farming?"

"Absolutely nothing." I'd spent all my life in Humboldt Park where any open space was covered with grass or concrete.

"What do you know about cows or corn or anything like that?" she asked.

"Nothing," I told her, "but I know something about obedience, and I believe God told me to buy a farm. Understanding can wait, but obedience can't."

The police commander's words had pierced my heart in the night. I knew God wanted me to use the property to care for the prostitutes and give them a safe place where God could turn their lives around, but I didn't know how any of this would happen.

A few days later, on Sunday morning, I stood in front of our congregation and told them, "Someone here has a farm, and God wants to use it to minister to prostitutes in our community." People looked at me with the same dumb-founded expression that Elizabeth had when I told her that God wanted us to buy a farm. These were people who had, like me, lived their entire lives in the city. They obviously thought I'd lost my mind. No one moved an inch.

The next Sunday, I made the same plea. No hand was raised. Weeks and months went by, and I didn't miss any opportunities to ask who had a farm we could use. I taught the story of Rahab and explained that she wasn't born a pros-titute, and she was redeemable by the grace of God. I even tried to put our congregation on a guilt trip: "With revela-tion comes responsibility. The police commander revealed the problem, and it's our responsibility to play a part in solving it. Come on. One of you has a farm God wants to use."

After eight months a lady in the church, Betty, came to me after the Sunday morning service and explained, "Pastor Choco, my uncle's wife passed away. He has a farm, and he thinks it might be what you're looking for." I was thrilled! She continued, "It's fifteen acres, in Cambridge, Illinois, which is three hours outside the city. He's willing to sell it to you for $160,000."

The farm was in Henry County. That probably doesn't mean anything to you, but Henry County is predominantly white. What would they think of a bunch of Puerto Rican do-gooders setting up shop in their neighborhood—and bringing prostitutes there?

The next morning, I visited the property with Elizabeth and our deacons. After I walked over the land and prayed, I came back to them and said, "Thus saith the Lord, 'This is the farm I have chosen.'" Then I told them, "So you will know that God is with us, He's going to send us all the money to buy it."

Over the next few days, I thought and prayed about how we could raise the money. The idea hit me that I could run and ride a bike from the farm to the church and have people commit to a certain dollar amount for every mile. The distance was exactly 182 miles. I figured it would take me three days to complete the jog and ride.

I set a date and asked people to pledge. In the meantime I had to train. Elizabeth told me, "Choco, you haven't run a mile in decades. If you try to run half of the way, you'll die!"

She had a point there. Ninety-one miles is a long way to run. Suddenly, riding the bike was looking awfully good.

I laughed. "Honey, don't you know that Jesus said if you try to preserve your life, you'll lose it, but if you'll lose it for His sake, you'll find it?" I asked.

I thought saying that would make her smile, but it didn't. I had to admit that she was right: I was woefully out of shape.

I started seriously training. Several months in I had another idea. I told a lady on our staff to go out on the streets and hire five prostitutes for an hour. I would pay them their normal rate. She knew I can be radical, but she thought this was over the top. We set a time for her to come back with them—seven o'clock that evening. Then she hopped in her car and drove off.

At precisely seven o'clock she came back to the church with five black and Hispanic women. I met them on the sidewalk. A couple of them were high on drugs, and all of them wore miniskirts. She introduced each of the women, explaining, "This one is charging $50, this one $40," and so on. The total was going to be $220. I paid them in cash.

With a look that was part smirk and part confusion, one of them asked, "What do you want us to do?"

I answered her, "I want you to follow me." I led them into the church and into a room that was set up as a banquet. We had a long table with a beautiful tablecloth, nice place settings, candles, and a red rose for each of them. Elizabeth was there to lead worship, and students in our Chicago Master's Commission came to perform a drama. I went to each chair by turn and held it for one of the five women to sit down. They looked very confused as a couple of church members set delicious plates of food in front of them.

As they began to eat, I explained, "We've bought your time for an hour, and during this time I want to tell you about a man named Jesus. He loves you dearly. We don't believe that you were born a prostitute. Jesus is the One who can change your life and give you hope and a future."

Elizabeth sang a couple of songs, and the students did a human video about God's love. I gave a message about God's love and forgiveness using the story of Rahab. At the end of an hour I told them, "Ladies, my time is up." By then all of them had tears streaming down their faces.

At that moment, one of the ladies stood and turned to me. "Nobody has ever treated us like this. We don't want your money, preacher." They were used to men using them. But this was different, and they could feel it. They had always performed to serve their johns, but we served them, loved them, and treated them with dignity. They put the money on the table—and insisted we keep it. I prayed for them, they got their roses, and our staff member took them back to the streets.

Before the police commander came to see me, the problem wasn't that I didn't care about women trapped in a lifestyle of prostitution, but I was so busy doing other things to help the people in our church grow that I was blind to what was happening on our street corners. I drove from our house to the church and back home every day, but I didn't really notice them before.

Now I noticed.

The leaks in the roof still needed to be fixed, and small group leaders still needed to be trained and equipped. But open eyes required open hearts and open wallets to care for "the least of these" in our neighborhood. When the condition of the community was made known to me, we had to act. I had to remove the spiritual blinders, see the hard reality, and take action.

God removed my blinders by sending a man, the police commander, to speak truth into my life, to be a light in my darkness, so I could see what was already there in plain sight. These women weren't just statistics; they're real people with real hurts and real hopes. Our dinner with them was just as important for us as it was for them. It showed that we could love them in a way that touched their hearts.

And what happened to the farm, which we decided to call New Life for Women?

A few men from our church and I did run and bike 182 miles, and I survived the ordeal, so I can write about it. We raised the money, bought the farm, and created a safe haven for women to get off the streets. We helped these ladies of the night find Christ, experience a loving, wholesome community, and embark on a new path for their lives. Looking back, throwing a banquet for five prostitutes was a message to them—and a message to me—that we were going to take action to care for them.

These days New Life for Women has made a difference in the lives of hundreds of women and their families. Elizabeth and I love to meet with the women there. Recently we held a chapel at the New Life for Women farm with some pastors from the Chicago area who wanted to see how God was working in the women's lives. We had a wonderful time of worship together, and then we began to share our testimonies. After Elizabeth and I talked about how we had come to faith in Jesus, we listened to the girls, one by one. I'll never forget the testimony of the last young woman. She told us, "Hello, my name is Lisa. I've been at the farm for five months. I'm not a victim anymore. When I first got here, all I talked about were all the bad things that happened to me. But today all I want to talk about is what God has done for me."

The atmosphere of the room changed as she spoke. I could feel the presence of God so real and so near. She continued, "But since you asked for my story, you need to know that my mother began sexually abusing me and prostituting me when I was five years old. I don't understand why she did that, but she seemed to like it."

My heart dropped. I couldn't imagine the pain and the shame of her life. She continued, "God is so good. I hear Him speaking to me, and I have a purpose now—I'm no longer a victim. I know that I'm supposed to be giving back. It would be easy to love and help the victims, women who have gone through experiences like mine, but this morning

God told me He wants me to love the abuser." At that moment, I felt what I can only describe as pure love.

At the end of chapel, I asked the girls if they had any questions. The young lady who had told us her story at the end asked me, "Pastor Choco, how do you do it? How do you love people who hurt you?"

I shared many of the thoughts that I talk about in this book, and I could tell she was listening intently. I had no doubt that God would show her the way.

SIT UP AND NOTICE

All of us have blind spots. They're not sins; they're part of being a flawed, limited human being. But they become sins when God uses someone to point them out to us and we refuse to admit them. It's a sin when we're comfortable with our preexisting point of view and we don't want any new information that challenges it. Just as God used the police commander to open my eyes, let me make a few observations that may open yours. We can identify a number of common blind spots in our relationships.

1. Superiority

We see our race, our education, our background, our status, or our peer group as better than others. We look down at people who aren't as nice or smart or noble or handsome or pretty or rich as we are. We believe our faith and our political positions are higher and better than the other side. I hear people mock as they call others bigots, which makes them bigoted about the bigots.

Increasingly in our culture people are getting their news from sources that validate what they already believe, a phenomenon called confirmation bias. They don't even entertain the thought that there might be another way to look at an issue. Every article and news program assures them they're right and the other side is wrong—no, not just wrong but evil. The issue may be racial injustice, masks, vaccines, immigration, guns, election results, or anything else—when we see ourselves as the guardians of truth and those who disagree as evil fools, we can't help but feel superior to them.

2. Entitlement

This is the assumption that "I deserve better." Sometimes it comes from want. We feel like victims, and we insist that someone step in to right the wrongs and fix the problems to make our lives better. Make no mistake, some people genuinely are victims. They've suffered injustice at the hands of family members, the police, or some other authority. Or perhaps they've lost their jobs— and maybe their homes— because of the pandemic and through no fault of their own. These people need our care and support as they come to grips with the reality of their loss, grieve their wounds, and heal. We need to distinguish between those who are actual victims and those who simply feel like victims because they've concluded they deserve better.

> Blind spots are not sins; they're part of being a flawed, limited human being. But they become sins when God uses someone to point them out to us and we refuse to admit them.

Other times, a sense of entitlement comes from a very different source: prosperity. We believe we've arrived socially and financially and we deserve only the finest treatment. For both groups entitlement thrives on comparison. The poor are upset because others have more than them, and the rich look at the ones who are even richer and conclude they have to have a better house, car, vacation, spouse, or some other mark of prestige to keep up.

At some point all of us need to face the stark reality that the only thing we deserve is judgment, but God has graciously given us His Son. Colossians 1:12 says He "has qualified [us] to share in the inheritance of the saints in light" (ESV). It's a gift, a grace gift, that should produce the deepest humility, the highest praise, and the most expansive gratitude. Drug addicts and prostitutes are well aware of where they've come from, but quite often, respectable, hardworking, bill-paying, God-fearing, middle-class people look at themselves and believe their current status is the result of their hard work and clean life. These are the ones who can easily forget they're desperately in need of God's great grace.

3. Suspicion

Since the pandemic began and the nation has suffered racial and political upheaval, people have even less trust in those who have authority, including leaders in business, politics, and the church. In an article on the erosion of trust in America today, David Brooks reports that the level of trust in our country has dropped by half in only a few decades. He explains, "Falling trust in institutions is bad enough; it's when people lose faith in each other that societies really begin to fall apart." He describes "our moment of moral convulsion" in the last decade by citing the political and social fragmentation. This, he says, was like an earthquake in our social fabric. And then, "the events of 2020—the coronavirus pandemic; the killing of George Floyd; militias, social-media mobs, and urban unrest—were like hurricanes that hit in the middle of that earthquake. They did not cause the moral convulsion, but they accelerated every trend. They flooded the ravines that had opened up in American society and exposed every flaw."[1] We're now more suspicious of anyone who isn't part of our self-reinforcing tribe.

When people feel overlooked or abused by those in authority, their trust is slowly eroded by constant, nagging disappointment or suddenly shattered by trauma. They learn to live in a world where they're always on guard, always have their antennae up to read people, and are always calculating their words and actions to keep from being hurt again. When they live in this world of suspicion, they question everyone's motives and assume those who disagree with them are fools. They don't realize that their fear and lack of trust have become completely normal.

Sometimes, of course, suspicions have their source in facts. Today, people of color are suspicious when a white policeman approaches them, abuse victims are wary of anyone with power, and people on each side of the political spectrum assume those on the other side are wrong and are trying to ruin the country.

In families, suspicion ruins relationships. I'm certainly not saying that it's wrong to be suspicious when there's good reason to wonder about people. But sometimes, suspicion takes on a life of its own, and no matter how much a spouse or growing child has proven to be trustworthy, unreasonable doubt poisons the connections.

4. Past wounds

For many people, past wounds color current relationships. Abuse, addiction, abandonment, divorce, death, disease, or some other problem caused deep hurts that haven't completely healed. One of the most common issues in marriage counseling is the impact of childhood trauma on the person's ability to give and receive love, to trust wisely, and to relax and be himself or herself. Blinders keep these individuals from seeing the enormity of the pain, but the blinders prevent healing. When these blinders are taken off, healing can begin, and relationships can become stronger than ever.

Deep hurts cloud our thinking and distort our vision. When I was a boy, our family suffered because of my father's drinking problem. We were a Catholic family, and one day when we were at a gathering, I saw the priest drink a beer with my dad. The priest may have been trying to connect with a man who needed Jesus, but that's not how I interpreted the scene. I believed he was betraying his calling and was no different than my father. He definitely wasn't helping my father or my family by encouraging his drinking, and at that moment, my trust in spiritual authority vanished. It took me a while to overcome that deep hurt and trust those in spiritual authority again.

5. Lost ground

Many Christians are outraged because they believe they're losing ground in the culture wars. Gay marriage has become the law of the land; abortion is widely accepted and in fact demanded by many in our country. Some are talking about overturning the second amendment about private ownership of guns, prayer has been taken out of schools, and religious liberties are under assault. As I write this chapter, our governor has just passed a law to mandate the teaching of LGBT history curriculum in public elementary schools in Illinois. A decade ago, who would have thought this would come about?

In the past, when Christians realized the nation was going in the wrong direction, they stood up and acted, leading the charge for change. Today, far too many of us remain immobile, unsure of what can be done, shackled by self-pity, and longing for someone else to change the trajectory of the nation.

In this cultural divide, I appreciate people on both sides who value integrity, compassion, and reason. It's wise to avoid the tribalism of insisting that our side is always right. Wise people are willing to listen to the points the other side is making, and they're willing to admit when their side is off base. Let me cite two writers who have the courage to criticize their own tribes.

First is Samuel Moyn, a professor of law and history at Yale University, with the liberal point of view. In an article titled, "We're in an Anti-liberal Moment. Liberals Need Better Answers," he explains how the modern concept of a liberal democracy has failed. He outlines some of the different views of liberals, and he comments, "But as the debate goes on, it will become clearer and clearer that the political system based on individual liberty and representative government doesn't need to be celebrated *or* repudiated. It needs to be saved from itself. Liberalism's adherents should be open to reimagining their tradition for a new era."

After a lengthy explanation of the history of the liberal cause, Moyn concludes that "liberalism's main problem" is that its vision of the good life has been corrupted by an overemphasis on economic freedom and an underemphasis on the spiritual and moral foundation of our culture. His solution is for liberals to move beyond dependence on God's truth and values.

> The right strategy for liberals is therefore to own their failure to make their ideals of self-creation a reality.

They must assert not merely that their tradition coex-
isted with and even promoted religious values—as it
undeniably did—but also revive their proposals for
meaningful life in the absence of divine superinten-
dence. Liberalism can thrive because it is the only
worldview so far that does not try to resolve the eternal
debate over whether to orient oneself to the divine, but
allows either bet to be made, and creative and meaningful lives to be led either way.[2]

No doubt, many who read this book would agree with
Moyn's assessment that liberalism has failed, but few would
agree with his prescription to fix the problem. This is only
one of the concerns conservatives have about liberal values
and policies.

A number of conservatives have the courage and the platform to critique the current state of the Republican Party.
One of these is David French, a former major in the Army
Reserve, a combat veteran of Iraq, and a former senior fellow
at the conservative National Review Institute. He is currently
the senior editor of *The Dispatch*, a conservative online magazine. French is also a committed Christian. In an article for
Time magazine, he laments the erosion of character among
white Evangelicals in America. He writes this:

Talk to engaged evangelicals, and fear is all too often
a dominant theme of their political life. The church is
under siege from a hostile culture...and there are reasons for evangelicals to be concerned. But there is no
reason for evangelicals to abandon long-held principles
to behave like any other political-interest group.

Instead, the evangelical church is called to be a
source of light in a darkening world. It is not given the

luxury of fear-based decisionmaking. Indeed, of all the groups in American life who believe they have the least to fear from American politics, Christians should top the list. The faithful should reject fear.[3]

In the last two thousand years, the church has thrived when it was persecuted and marginalized. Today, those who expect to be given preferential treatment rise up in self-righteous anger and wallow in self-pity. That's not the way of Jesus!

I need to say it again: I'm certainly not suggesting that we just cave in and give up our moral positions on the wide range of issues. It's our responsibility to stand up for justice, righteousness, and kindness, but we stand in the name of Jesus, not in the name of a political party or a political leader. And we trust in Jesus, not the party or the leader, to give us wisdom, direction, and perseverance to fight the good fight.

> Being a Christian with convictions doesn't give us a green light to voice those convictions with venom in our voices.

Being a Christian with convictions doesn't give us a green light to voice those convictions with venom in our voices. Jesus pleaded with the Pharisees to experience the Father's affection. And I think He is pleading with us so we will serve Him with a beautiful blend of strong convictions, deep gratitude, and genuine love for people who disagree.

REALITY AND HOPE

We need to wake up and realize Christians are no longer in the driver's seat in our culture. Our voice is waning, but it isn't silent. Some Christian leaders on the liberal side have joined the chorus against faith and values. Some conservatives have thrown their hands up in despair and headed for the sidelines. But there's another way to respond. Like we saw in the last chapter with the Jews in Babylon, we can engage people, get to know people on every side of the issues, build friendships, speak the truth with love, and form an alternate society fueled by Jesus' love instead of self-pity and anger.

For years, that's what I tried to do at New Life Covenant in Humboldt Park. In addition, the church has partnered with many others around the country and the world who want to be known as loving, reasonable, practical, and kind members of society. We need to get it into our hearts that we represent Jesus more than we represent a political party.

At this point in history, we're at a defining moment for individuals, churches, and denominations. Our supreme loyalty is being tested. Fear isn't a sustaining emotion; love is. Choose love. Our situation may appear to be precarious, but it isn't. The Bible gives us immense hope. We need to remember that at the end of the story, we win. Don't get bent out of shape by setbacks and opposition. That's the environment where Jesus demonstrated His love, and it's the situation when Paul learned to remain strong in his faith.

> We need to get it into our hearts that we represent Jesus more than we represent a political party.

I love the example Jehoshaphat gave us when he faced combined armies arrayed against the Jewish nation. He called the people of Judah together to fast and pray, and then he stood before them and prayed.

LORD, the God of our ancestors, are you not the God who is in heaven? You rule over all the kingdoms of the nations. Power and might are in your hand, and no one can withstand you. Our God, did you not drive out the inhabitants of this land before your people Israel and give it forever to the descendants of Abraham your friend? They have lived in it and have built in it a sanctuary for your Name, saying, "If calamity comes upon us, whether the sword of judgment, or plague or famine, we will stand in your presence before this temple that bears your Name and will cry out to you in our distress, and you will hear us and save us."

—2 CHRONICLES 20:6–9

Jehoshaphat recounted the reality of the problem they faced. Then a prophet stood in the assembly with a word from God. He told them, "Do not be afraid or discouraged because of this vast army. For the battle is not yours, but God's.... Take up your positions; stand firm and see the deliverance the LORD will give you, Judah

> Fear isn't a sustaining emotion; love is. Choose love.

and Jerusalem. Do not be afraid; do not be discouraged. Go out to face them tomorrow, and the LORD will be with you" (vv. 15, 17). The people were encouraged. They sang praises to God, and they marched toward the battlefield. When they got there, God had already defeated the armies, and the people took three days to gather all the equipment left behind.

That's the model for us as we face the hostile armies against us. Instead of giving up or getting angry or fearful, we can fast and pray and, together, trust God to do what only He can do. The victory may not happen quickly or as dramatically as it did for Jehoshaphat and his people, but God will prevail sooner or later. This confidence in Him should enable us to relax, lower our blood pressure, and engage people with love and understanding instead of assuming we have to conquer them. The historian concludes, "The fear of God came on all the surrounding kingdoms when they heard how the LORD had fought against the enemies of Israel. And the kingdom of Jehoshaphat was at peace, for his God had given him rest on every side" (vv. 29–30).

URGENCY AND COMPASSION

The Epistle to the Romans is the most comprehensive explanation of the gospel and its implications in the New Testament. In chapter 10, Paul comes back to the offer God makes to every person: "Everyone who calls on the name of the Lord will be saved" (v. 13). But Paul knows that God has given us the ministry of reconciliation, so he asks:

> How, then, can they call on the one they have not believed in? And how can they believe in the one of whom they have not heard? And how can they hear without someone preaching to them? And how can anyone preach unless they are sent? As it is written: "How beautiful are the feet of those who bring good news!"
>
> —ROMANS 10:14–15

People have an urgent need for us to tell them about Jesus, but urgency must be combined with kindness. We see this blend in John's account of Jesus in Samaria. He begins this story with a strange statement: "Now [Jesus] had to go through Samaria" (John 4:4). The Jews and Samaritans hated each other. Jews went out of their way to avoid even seeing a

Samaritan, and when they traveled between north and south, they usually went thirty miles out of the way to avoid passing through Samaria. But Jesus had a different purpose. His goal wasn't to condemn Samaritans or to avoid them. He loved them and wanted to engage them, so He determined "to go through Samaria."

The story is very familiar. When He came to Sychar, He stopped at a well. He sent the twelve disciples into town to buy food. (Imagine sending twelve to buy food for thirteen people! It was obvious He didn't want them around for a while.) After they left, a woman came to the well at midday. This, too, was strange because women drew water first thing each morning. This woman came later because she was an outcast among her peers.

Jesus asked her for a drink of water, and this initiated the longest conversation with Jesus recorded in the Bible. It's a sensitive but frank discussion. Jesus loved her enough to be there when others had rejected her, but He also spoke the truth about her spiritual condition. He didn't let social barriers stop Him. In their conversation, Jesus offered her "living water." She probably was sure that He wouldn't make such an offer if He knew about her sexual past, but then He said He knew all about it! Jesus knew the worst about her, but He still made the offer of a cleansing flood. He was fully aware of her deepest sins and darkest secrets, but He loved her anyway. She was so excited that she went into town and told everyone she knew about Jesus! His unconditional love filled her with soul-satisfying grace—that's living water. (See John 4:5–30.)

We feel safer behind physical or psychological barriers, but Jesus tore them down so He could connect with people. In the same way, Jesus wants us to become friends with gay people, black people, brown people, white people, old people, young people, rich people, poor people, sick people, healthy people, hard-to-love people—all kinds of people from all walks of life. To Jesus, things like this didn't matter at all. And they shouldn't stop us from extending love either.

Quite often, we want to protect ourselves and look strong to the people in our circle, but Jesus was vulnerable. He was willing to take the heat for loving outcasts, Samaritans, lepers, women, children, sick people, lame people, tax collectors, prostitutes, thieves, and Romans. (I'm sure I left out someone, but you get the idea.)

> We feel safer behind physical or psychological barriers, but Jesus tore them down so He could connect with people.

In her book *Daring Greatly: How the Courage to Be Vulnerable Transforms the Way We Live, Love, Parent, and Lead*, professor and author Brené Brown states that self-protection is the opposite of love. Vulnerability requires everything we've got, but it opens the door to the kind of love we're talking about in this book. She writes:

> Vulnerability is the birthplace of love, belonging, joy, courage, empathy, and creativity. It is the source of hope, empathy, accountability, and authenticity. If we want greater clarity in our purpose or deeper and more meaningful spiritual lives, vulnerability is the path.... Vulnerability sounds like truth and feels like courage. Truth and courage aren't always comfortable, but they're never weakness.[4]

Jesus made Himself vulnerable to identify with the marginalized and the poor. When someone asked about taxes, He had to ask someone to give Him a coin. He was, as pastor Tim Keller said, "a King without a quarter." When He rode into Jerusalem, He rode on a borrowed donkey, He had dinner with His disciples in a borrowed room, and He was buried in a borrowed tomb. And He identified with the oppressed: He was arrested on trumped-up charges, tried in a kangaroo court, lashed without mercy, and killed even though He was innocent.[5] At any moment, He could have stopped it all. He could have completely wiped out the human race, but instead, He submitted to the injustice and torture. Dying in our place was the only way for Him to fulfill the Father's plans.

Loving our enemies—and the undocumented, protesters, those who burned courthouses after George Floyd's death, those who stormed the Capitol, Republicans, Democrats, people who defend those we consider indefensible, outcasts, people who have a way of getting under our

> Self-protection is the opposite of love. Vulnerability requires everything we've got, but it opens the door to the kind of love we're talking about.

skin, and every other person we are tempted to categorize as "them"—doesn't happen because we grit our teeth and choose to be loving, just, and generous. It happens when we are overwhelmed with the incredible truth that Jesus became supremely vulnerable so that we could be loved, safe, and secure in His arms. That's the gospel. That's the message that changes hearts and gives us the desire and will to love people we find unlovely.

When Jesus stood on the hilltop before the Ascension, He gave His disciples their marching orders: to take the message of God's grace, hope, and love to every corner of the globe and get involved in the lives of new believers to help them grow into fully devoted followers of Christ.

Every corner of the globe? Yes, every corner. Not just people who are like us but, specifically, those who aren't like us. This wasn't the Great Suggestion. It's the Great Commission, which reflects God's heart and defines our purpose. We simply can't (and won't) reach people with the gospel of grace if we insist on remaining at arm's length from them, if we despise them, if we feel superior to them, or if we ignore them. We need to be strong enough in our faith to become gentle. If we aren't caring, kind, and compassionate toward people who are overlooked or condemned, we're demonstrating that we're weak in our faith and we haven't really experienced the love of Jesus.

SEEING AND ACTING

When the police commander walked into my office and told me about the hundreds of arrests of prostitutes in our neighborhood, my eyes were opened. Had I noticed them before? Certainly, but I'd never really *seen* them before that day. Objectivity requires responsibility, and God led us to buy a farm and launch a ministry to care for these ladies and help them chart a new path for their

> If we aren't caring, kind, and compassionate toward people who are overlooked or condemned, we're demonstrating that we're weak in our faith and we haven't really experienced the love of Jesus.

future. I've seen God open the eyes of a lot of people, and they've taken action.

Richard is a prominent attorney who was living the good life, making a lot of money, and enjoying the prestige of his success. One day, a friend who had been visiting a death-row inmate asked Richard if he would be willing to visit another man on death row. Richard could think of a dozen reasons why he didn't want to spend a day driving two hours to the prison, meeting with a man who had no future, and driving back. But after the third request, he agreed to go "and give it a try."

The prisoner his friend had picked out for him was his polar opposite: John was a black man who had murdered two people, had no more appeals, and was waiting on the state to give him an execution date. But John wasn't at all what Richard expected. He had become a Christian, and he wanted to talk to Richard about the joy he'd found in Jesus. They spoke together for two hours, and Richard knew he would go back again to see his new friend.

The environment of the visit was oppressive: a walk past high walls and a double fence of concertina wire, then down a long hallway to the room where prisoners were behind thick windows. Conversations were held on the phones hanging on the walls. Still, John and Richard made a real connection. When he walked out of the prison, Richard could feel the sense of relief to be out of there. But he realized John felt the oppression every day and to a far greater extent.

Richard went back to see John the next month and the next and the next. For ten years, the two very unlikely friends encouraged each other. Richard was in the observation room when John was strapped to the gurney and was given the medications that would stop his heart. Before he died, he thanked Richard for being his friend. Thinking back to their first visit ten years earlier, Richard knew he had been blind to the loneliness and heartache of those who were waiting on death row. Meeting John opened his eyes.

Aaliyah had every reason to be guarded. Her mother got pregnant with her when she was only fourteen, and of course, a child doesn't know how to raise a child. Her birth father was never in the picture. When her mother had another child, Aaliyah effectively became a mom to her younger sister. Her mom left home when Aaliyah was nine years old, and at that time, Aaliyah and her sister moved in with their grandmother.

Even as a young girl, she tried to numb her anger with drinking and drugs. Her mother came back when Aaliyah was thirteen, and she returned with a newborn baby. This made Aaliyah even more resentful. She wondered how her mother could come back and care for a new baby when she hadn't cared for her and her sister.

Soon, her mother had a number of men coming in and out of the house, creating a volatile, toxic environment. One of the "boyfriends" tried to sexually assault Aaliyah, so she told her mother, "Either he goes or I go." Her mother chose the guy, so Aaliyah left.

Aaliyah drifted from house to house among her friends, but finally a lady in her church told her about the Teen Center, which is part of our church's Dream Center. Even though she occasionally went to church, Aaliyah didn't believe in God. She couldn't imagine a God who would let her go through so much pain. She agreed to go to the Teen Center, and the love she experienced there has transformed her life. Her deep wounds have been touched by God's kindness, the leaders of the Teen Center have given her a safe place, and she has a new, powerful purpose.

For Aaliyah, the blind spot was her belief that no one was safe and everyone was out to use her or harm her. She didn't trust anyone, so she didn't believe anyone would ever care for her or even give a rip about her. At the Teen Center, though, the blinders came off as love flooded her heart. She attended our three-year Master's Commission, and she has grown tremendously in her faith. The pain from her past has given her enormous compassion for others who are hurting, abused, and abandoned. She realizes God uses people to communicate His love to her, and now she's a channel of love to other young women who have lost hope.

After God gave me the vision to buy a farm where ladies of the evening could find forgiveness, healing, and hope, He brought in the money to create the facilities, and then we needed a couple to be the leaders at New Life for Women—to become the loving, strong parents these ladies never had. I talked to a couple who were longtime members of our church and asked them to be the pastors at the farm. Their first names were Rico and Alice. I wasn't shy. I said to them, "I'm asking you to play this role for ten years."

I chose Rico and Alice because I knew they could identify with these women. In their dark past Rico had been in prison, and Alice had been in rehab. When she entered the program, she had to put her two children into a foster program. When Alice got out of the program, she was reunited with her kids. Rico soon got out of prison, and both of them got saved.

This couple made incredible progress in overcoming their

past and built a new, productive life together. They were exactly the kind of people these women needed at the farm. The ladies loved Rico like a father and Alice like a mother. When he died, the ladies who had been at the farm came to the funeral and wept for the man who had treated them with dignity and love.

Years before, when Rico was in prison and Alice was in rehab, they had a blind spot about their future. They could barely imagine getting out and getting clean. The idea that God could use them—and specifically use the lessons they'd learned from their biggest struggles—to turn around the lives of young women would have seemed absurd to them. But it wasn't absurd to God. When He reveals the truth and takes the blinders off our eyes, we have the responsibility to step up and step into the lives of people we may have noticed but we have never really seen before.

Since love is the currency of the kingdom, God's bank account of love is enormous. But far too few of us make significant withdrawals. We live at the poverty level, barely remaining civil much of the time and delighting when we hear that those we don't like have been set back, hurt, or shamed. When that happens, we've gone to the wrong bank. We spend our time withdrawing anger, resentment, superiority, suspicion, and entitlement, but those withdrawals leave us emotionally and spiritually impoverished.

> God's bank account of love is enormous. But far too few of us make significant withdrawals.

Take the blinders off. See people the way Jesus sees them. Withdraw love from the vast store of compassion you find in Him, and invest that love into the lives of every person you meet.

DISCUSSION QUESTIONS

- Describe a time when someone spoke truth to you about a blind spot. What was it? How did you respond? How do you wish you had responded?

- This chapter describes a number of factors that can cause us to be blinded: superiority, entitlement, suspicion, past wounds and betrayal, and fear of losing ground. Which of these rings true for you as an excuse to ignore or reject people instead of reaching out to them?

- How would you define and describe confirmation bias? Do you think you're affected by it? Explain your answer.

- How are love and vulnerability connected? What are some reasons we don't want to be vulnerable? How does Jesus' vulnerability touch your heart, change your perspective, and motivate you to action? (Or does it?)

- Whom is someone you know who has taken bold steps to draw on the currency of the kingdom?

- Read 2 Chronicles 20:5–17, 29–30. Describe Jehoshaphat's response when he saw the reality of the armies marching against his nation. How is this an example for you and me?

ACTION POINT: WHAT LOVE LOOKS LIKE

Ask the most objective person who knows you well this striking question: "Do you see a blind spot in me about loving people who disagree with me?" And listen without defending yourself. In fact, after listening for a while, ask, "Will you tell me more about that?" And listen again.

CHAPTER 5

"FOLLOW ME"

IN THE 2019 election in Chicago, Lori Lightfoot was elected mayor. She is the first openly lesbian mayor in our city. Soon after the election, she held a celebration for her most significant donors at a high-rise condo smack-dab in the center of the city. Only thirty people received invitations, and to my surprise I was one of them. I was surprised because I never donated to her campaign.

Before she arrived, I introduced myself to people and shook their hands. As we got to know each other, I found that they were the power brokers for the liberal community in Chicago. All of them were 100 percent supportive of her and everything she stood for. If they'd had flags, they'd have had two: blue (as part of blue-state America) and rainbow-colored (for gay pride). Very few, if any, of the other twenty-nine people in the room knew who I was or what I did. We were from two different worlds.

As I stood in the room talking with the new mayor's supporters, I thought, "What am I doing here? I don't belong in this group. I'm a fish out of water." But I quickly realized it was good and right for me to be present. The church needs to show up and represent Jesus to every person everywhere.

As the new mayor arrived and greeted guests one by one around the room, one of her staff members introduced me. "This is Reverend De Jesús," she said.

Ms. Lightfoot's eyes met mine. She smiled, and her face lit up. "I know who you are!"

"Mayor-elect, congratulations on your victory," I told her. "I want you to know that I'm ready to work with you to address the problem of crime and violence in our great city."

I opened our relationship by bringing up an issue I was sure we could agree on. I wanted the new mayor to know that I was not furious that she was elected and wasn't afraid to talk to her about the things that matter to God. That night wasn't the time to get into policies and values; that time would come sooner or later. Someone took a picture of the two of us, and before long, the gathering was over.

A week after I met the mayor-elect, representatives of President Trump's White House Opportunity and Revitalization Council came to Chicago to meet with me. For the past two years, I had sat down with several of these officials in Washington and in Chicago. We met at our church with about fifteen other pastors and church leaders. The members of the council explained the president's agenda to bring life to dying areas of cities, revitalize schools that are closing, and find solutions to the rampant crime that often accompanies the decay of urban environments.

I'm sure some people would be horrified by the fact that I met with a lesbian new mayor of the city in a room filled with people from the political left. And I'm sure others would be equally outraged that I met with representatives of a man who has shown contempt for immigrants. That's fine. Each side can be upset with me. I'm just following the example of Jesus by reaching out to people all across the spectrum to love them where they are. I don't have to agree with people to have a relationship with them, and I don't have to demand they change for us to have a meaningful connection.

FOOTSTEPS

When Jesus called the disciples to follow Him, He didn't take them to a meeting room in a church. He took them to the streets, the highways, and the fields to find people and tell them about God's love. And He didn't just tell them about the Father's love; He genuinely loved them.

The Gospel writers give us a wide range of scenes in which Jesus took action to love people: He touched lepers, let a prostitute pour perfume on His feet, invited Himself to dinner with a hated tax collector, accepted an invitation to dinner with a Pharisee, and watched as four men dug a hole in the roof to lower their paralyzed friend in front of Him.

He met with Nicodemus, the powerful Pharisee, and He stopped to cast a demon out of a man who was naked and living in a cemetery. He loved the Jews, but He also loved the Samaritans and Romans. He enjoyed the comforts of home with His friends, Mary, Martha, and Lazarus, but He also suffered the condemnation and rejection of the people in His hometown. He held little children in His arms, and He corrected the misguided thinking of people who wanted bread more than they wanted the Bread of Life. Jesus came for the rich and the poor, the religious and the irreligious. All of these people need God's love; no one is off-limits or is too far gone. Today, He still comes for them, but let me remind you that He uses our faces, voices, and arms.

To be honest, it was as hard for the disciples to grasp the love of Jesus as it is for us today—and Jesus was right in front of them! Three of them had gone to the mountain with Jesus when His appearance changed and His garments glowed. Moses and Elijah appeared with Him in splendor. What a sight! When they came down from the mountain, the disciples watched as Jesus cast a demon out of a boy as his worried father looked on. But instead of being amazed that Jesus used all His power to love the people around Him, they argued about who would be the greatest in His kingdom. They were jockeying for position as they watched Jesus humble Himself to love, give, and serve.

> Jesus came for the rich and the poor, the religious and the irreligious. All of these people need God's love; no one is off-limits or is too far gone.

Then, as the time approached for Him to be arrested, unjustly tried, convicted, and executed, they traveled through a Samaritan village. When the people there didn't welcome Jesus, James and John (two of the disciples closest to Jesus) asked Him, "Lord, do you want us to call fire down from heaven and destroy them?"

Jesus let them know it wasn't (and still isn't) His purpose to incinerate every person who opposes Him. (See Luke 9:51–56.)

WHATEVER IT TAKES

As we've seen, our love can be dried up by a feeling of superiority, undisguised resentment, and other factors, but we can also become complacent and assume we've earned some comfort. We can say, "Look at all I've done for people. That's enough, isn't it?"

Early in His ministry, Jesus was very popular. People brought their family members and friends to Him to be healed. One time, in the middle of this success, He got up very early and went out to pray. When the sun came up, the disciples were excited about another day of great miracles and popularity. They went to look for Him, and when they found Him, they exclaimed, "Everyone is looking for you!" (Mark 1:37).

Jesus answered them, "Let us go somewhere else—to the nearby villages—so I can preach there also. That is why I have come" (v. 38). Nothing could stop Jesus from loving people who hadn't yet experienced the wonder of His kindness and compassion. Jesus wasn't looking for popularity, and His success wasn't measured by how big the miracle or the crowd was. He was searching for individuals to love.

We have a divided world today, but it's no worse than Palestine in the first century. The Jews despised both the Samaritans and the Romans. The Zealots believed that armed revolt was the only solution to Roman occupation. The Essenes tried to flee the oppression by creating a community far out in the desert. The Pharisees assumed if they could follow God's laws well enough, surely He would send the Messiah to conquer the Romans. And the Sadducees collaborated with the Romans to share power and lower the level of tension. Instead of two parties that don't trust each other, they had four! (And that doesn't include the Romans.) But none of them understood that the Messiah was right in the midst of them and that He had a different solution in mind.

People were stunned that Jesus reached out past social norms to care for people who were considered unclean and despicable. He didn't give a rip what others said. He just loved people and took action to care for them. When He touched the leper, the people watching were undoubtedly horrified. They'd never do anything like that! Well, that's not entirely true. Some of the people watching were other lepers, and they were amazed that a religious leader would make Himself unclean by being loving enough to touch one of their own. If He would do that for one, maybe...

One time, I went to the hospital to visit a man in our church who was dying from HIV/AIDS. As I stood at the door of his room, the nurse asked, "Pastor, do you want to wear gloves? You don't want to take any chances."

I looked at his emaciated figure in the bed. By this time, he was awake, but he was intubated so he couldn't talk. A half-dozen medical machines were hooked up to him, and his wife was sitting quietly next to him. The doctors had told them he had only days to live. In response to the nurse, I shook my head. "No, I won't be wearing gloves."

He needed a human touch. I didn't want any guardedness on my part to mar one of his last moments on earth. I held his hand. I reminded him of the glory he was about to enter, and I prayed for him. He was surprised that I wasn't wearing gloves. The look on his face was how I imagine the look on the leper's face when Jesus touched him.

In Paul's letter to the Romans, he asks, "Who shall separate us from the love of Christ? Shall trouble or hardship or persecution or famine or nakedness or danger or sword?" (8:35). Let me add this thought: "Shall being a Republican or a Democrat, being a citizen or undocumented, being gay or straight, being a tough guy or a feminist, or having any other belief or lifestyle cause Jesus to stop loving us?"

The answer is no, and if we claim to follow Him, nothing will stop us from loving people too.

LOSE YOUR LIFE

Every person is born self-absorbed, but that's because it's our nature to be selfish. This inbred bent is inflamed by our consumer culture. The ads we see and hear promise that the next purchase will give us ultimate fulfillment—and that's what we think is the good life: having everything we want and avoiding everything that's annoying or painful.

But Jesus came not to be served but to serve. No one took His life; He freely gave it. The Pharisees and the Romans played only bit parts in the drama. His reason for coming to earth was to die a shameful death so we could receive forgiveness, honor, and adoption into God's family. In one of the most powerful statements in the Gospels, Jesus said these words to those who were committed to follow Him:

> Whoever wants to be my disciple must deny themselves and take up their cross and follow me. For whoever wants to save their life will lose it, but whoever loses their life for me will find it. What good will it be for someone to gain the whole world, yet forfeit their soul? Or what can anyone give in exchange for their soul? For the Son of Man is going to come in his Father's glory with his angels, and then he will reward each person according to what they have done.
>
> —MATTHEW 16:24–27

Jesus gives us a cost-benefit analysis. If we organize our pursuits around our own pleasure, prestige, and power, we'll live with the nagging fear that we'll never have enough. We'll compare ourselves with others, and we'll believe that we aren't handsome enough, pretty enough, smart enough, talented enough, or rich enough.

But if we say no to selfish ambition and yes to Jesus' purpose, we'll organize our lives around Him—His love, His power, His timetable, and His goals. And we'll experience the joy of knowing the God of glory, the love of the One who gave everything for us, and the power of the Spirit as we align our purposes with His. Who is the one who puts money into ventures that are guaranteed losses? That's a foolish person. But who is the one who invests in ventures that have guaranteed profits? That's a wise person.

Jesus doesn't force us to lay down our selfish ambitions and follow Him. It's our choice—and the results are our consequences. If we demand our own way, we'll follow our desires and emotions. Our anger at anyone who gets in our way gives us an adrenaline rush, but it eats us alive. On the other hand, if we want to play it safe and avoid risks, we'll miss out on the blessings God has for us.

In the classic movie *Forrest Gump*, a hurricane threatened the shrimp boat fleet. Forrest and Lieutenant Dan took their boat out into the sea to ride out the wind and the waves, but the other captains tied their boats to the docks. The next morning after the storm had passed, when Forrest and Dan brought their boat back to the harbor, they saw that all the sea vessels were destroyed. Playing it safe had cost them everything.

For Forrest and Dan, what had seemed like a reckless

decision to move into the storm saved their boat. That's a message for each Christian and for the church at large. If we try to protect ourselves from the storms in our culture, we'll be destroyed. But if we launch out into the storm in the ship of God's great love, we'll have the buoyancy to stay afloat and live to love another day.

The kingdom of God is upside down: If we lose our lives for Jesus' sake, we'll find real life. But if we cling to our selfish ambitions and live to protect ourselves from risks, we'll lose the joy and impact God created us for. This is entirely countercultural. When we follow Jesus, we choose Him and His values and purposes over everything the world promises. We're willing to lose opportunities, our reputations, and our comfort so Jesus' kingdom will be advanced. We're willing to love when it's unpopular and inconvenient. People will post ugly comments about us on social media. They'll gossip about us, make fun of us, and avoid us. When we read the accounts of Jesus' life, we get vivid reminders that His love was terribly unpopular with the religious elite, and it proved to be far more than inconvenient—it cost Him His life.

The men and women in our Rose of Sharon ministry sacrifice every Friday night to go out to the streets to meet prostitutes. They give each lady a rose and tell her, "This is what Jesus thinks of you. You're as precious as this rose." And they pray for these ladies. If you ask this team how they feel about losing their Friday nights for the sake of Christ, they'll laugh at the thought. This is what they live for! Bringing light into the darkness of these lives gives them the deepest sense of fulfillment: they're doing what Jesus would do, with the love He has for all people, with no strings attached. Many of the women who have come to the New Life for Women farm are the direct result of this team's love.

Loving people is often complicated. Miriam is one of the ladies who came to the farm in the first years it was open. She went there to turn her life around, but the tug of her old life was strong. She kept threatening to leave the farm and go back to the streets of Chicago. She remembers, "Oh my, I fought with Pastor Rico all the time, but he never stopped loving me."

One day she told another lady that she was going to take one of the bikes they used for exercise and ride all the way back to the city. The lady told Pastor Rico about Miriam's plan, so he let the air out of the tires of all the bikes and chained them together. When Miriam saw the locked-up bikes with flat tires, she wasn't angry. In fact she laughed

> But if we cling to our selfish ambitions and live to protect ourselves from risks, we'll lose the joy and impact God created us for.

because she realized Pastor Rico had gone to great lengths to keep her around, and she felt loved.

When we say no to our selfish desires and yes to Jesus, we get in touch with the heart of love, we obey the command to love, and we realize the emptiness of not loving—and God uses us to give hope to the hopeless, courage to the timid, and security to the fearful.

THE HEART OF LOVE

As we've seen, we can't manufacture kindness, compassion, and empathy. We can only draw from what's deposited in the bank of our hearts. Love is never bankrupt. When some people go to their banks to withdraw happiness, they discover they've spent years depositing resentment and self-pity. They didn't deposit nearly enough love.

But love isn't the only thing worth depositing. God wants to put justice, righteousness, and kindness into the account as well. In his famous "I Have a Dream" speech, civil rights leader Martin Luther King Jr. proclaimed, "But we refuse to believe that the bank of justice is bankrupt. We refuse to believe that there are insufficient funds in the great vaults of opportunity of this nation. And so we've come to cash this check, a check that will give us upon demand the riches of freedom and the security of justice."[1] Dr. King was committed to the values of God's kingdom making a difference in the lives of people throughout our country. That's my commitment too, but it won't happen if our hearts are bankrupt.

In his letter to the Ephesians, Paul is brutally honest about what the culture deposits in our hearts and our natural response to it: "Get rid of all bitterness, rage and anger, brawling and slander, along with every form of malice" (4:31). These actions grieve the Holy Spirit and short-circuit God's purposes for us. Instead, he tells us, "Be kind and compassionate to one another, forgiving each other, just as in Christ God forgave you" (v. 32). We can be kind and com-

> We can't manufacture kindness, compassion, and empathy. We can only draw from what's deposited in the bank of our hearts.

passionate only to the extent we've experienced the kindness and compassion of Jesus. And our willingness and capacity to forgive those who have offended us is determined by the depth of our grasp of God's forgiveness for our sins. In other words, if we're not kind, compassionate, or forgiving, we need God to do a work in our hearts.

But Paul isn't finished with his explanation about the heart of love. He continues, "Follow God's example, therefore, as dearly loved children and walk in the way of love, just as Christ loved us and gave himself up for us as a fragrant offering and sacrifice to God" (5:1–2). How much does Christ love us? He gave up the comfort and glory of heaven to come to earth, to identify with us, and to give everything for us. That's "the way of love," and that's the example God gives us. When our bank is full, the withdrawals look like Jesus. When our bank is empty of God's love, the only things that come out are comparison, competition, resentment, anger, and self-pity.

What's in your heart's bank?

THE COMMAND TO LOVE

Loving others isn't optional. And loving people who don't love us isn't secondary to the call of God. It's the essential nature of a person whose heart is full of His love. God gives us clear directives to love people. The Great Commandment is to love God first and then love our neighbor. Jesus told His disciples to love as He had loved them. That's a tall order! And in his first letter, the apostle John makes the connection between the fact of God's love and our obligation to love others.

> Dear friends, let us love one another, for love comes from God. Everyone who loves has been born of God and knows God. Whoever does not love does not know God, because God is love. This is how God showed his love among us: He sent his one and only

Son into the world that we might live through him. This is love: not that we loved God, but that he loved us and sent his Son as an atoning sacrifice for our sins. Dear friends, since God so loved us, we also ought to love one another. No one has ever seen God; but if we love one another, God lives in us and his love is made complete in us.

—1 JOHN 4:7–12

Did you catch that? Those who don't love show that they don't know God. Love is the primary characteristic of the believer, and it's the kind of love that doesn't have requirements, doesn't demand compliance, doesn't have limitations, and always does what's best for the other person. John is writing specifically to the family of God, and goodness knows, we have enough trouble loving each other! But the quality and extent of love goes far beyond the walls of our churches and into every corner of our communities.

> Loving people who don't love us isn't secondary to the call of God. It's the essential nature of a person whose heart is full of His love.

God has given us a script for our role in the grand drama of His plan to redeem the world. Our first act is to respond with humility and gratitude to the love of Jesus, then to love the people in the family of God. If we do that, others in the world will see this love and be attracted to the main character, Jesus. All of us are actors on the stage. Our love for each other is on display all day every day. What are they seeing? God's love in our hearts.

THE EMPTINESS OF NOT LOVING

Judy, a young woman who is now part of our church, told Elizabeth her story of political activism. Years ago, she was outraged at the lack of effort on the part of politicians to address injustice. She was so passionate that she devoted her life to the cause. She married a man who had the same passions, and they decided they didn't want to have children because the kids would distract them from their zeal. But Judy found Christ, and she soon realized much of her passion had been misdirected. She thought the intensity of her emotion gave her credibility, but her fervor for social activism left her empty, wondering what she'd missed.

> Love is the primary characteristic of the believer, and it's the kind of love that doesn't have requirements, doesn't demand compliance, doesn't have limitations, and always does what's best for the other person.

It's easy for us to be passionate about a cause but miss the heart of God. In Paul's first letter to the Christians in Corinth, he has a long explanation about the body of Christ and the gifts of the Spirit. Sandwiched in the middle of this teaching is his famous chapter on love. We often use this chapter in weddings, and people sigh when they hear it read. But that's not the response of the Corinthians when they heard Paul's letter! He begins, "If I speak in the tongues of men or of angels, but do not have love, I am only a resounding gong or a clanging cymbal" (1 Cor. 13:1). The Corinthians bragged about their supernatural gifts and competed with each other for attention. Paul was telling them that practicing the gifts without love is no better than the noise made by the priests in pagan temples.

Then he writes, "If I have the gift of prophecy and can fathom all mysteries and all knowledge, and if I have a faith that can move mountains, but do not have love, I am nothing" (v. 2). In other words, if we have fantastic leadership gifts and see wonderful results but we don't exhibit a life of love, it doesn't count for anything. It may look like a big score, but it's a big fat zero in God's eyes.

But Paul isn't finished. He understood that religious zeal can be a way to get attention and win power over others, so he warns, "If I give all I possess to the poor and give over my body to hardship that I may boast, but do not have love, I gain nothing" (v. 3). Extreme generosity means nothing without love. Total dedication is an illusion without love. His point in all three verses is that we can be very busy—and very effective—in serving in church, but if it's not out of a heart of love, then the experience leaves us empty.

Let me go back to Judy's story. She and her husband got involved in our church, and Judy's experience with running political rallies was valuable to the women's ministry events. After the first one, she remarked that the spirit of our planning meetings was completely different from the ones she had worked on in the political arena. She said Elizabeth's team listened to each other, disagreed respectfully, and supported each other when decisions were made. She noted the stark contrast with the yelling, cursing, and blaming that characterized many of the political planning meetings. They had passion but without love. They had talents but without love. They were radically devoted to a cause but without love. And it showed.

When Judy realized the emptiness of her life before, she cried, but they were tears of joy and thankfulness. These days, she and her husband have two beautiful children, and their family basks in the love of Jesus. Judy and her husband serve, and they serve passionately, but they are motivated by the life-changing love of God.

THE MARK OF AUTHENTICITY

John was so overwhelmed by the love of Jesus that in his Gospel, he called himself "the disciple whom Jesus loved." That doesn't mean Jesus didn't love the others, but the strong tenderness of Jesus was so wonderful to John that it became the source of his identity.

John gave us another picture of someone who was overcome with the love of Jesus. When Mary and Martha's brother, Lazarus, got sick, they sent for Jesus to come and heal him. Jesus had more in mind than healing him, however. He delayed His journey until His friend had been dead and in the grave for four days, and then He showed up. The miracle of raising Lazarus from the dead thrilled the people who were watching, and we can imagine what it meant to the sisters.

The next scene in John's account is at a dinner thrown for Jesus as a celebration. Martha, as we might have guessed, was busy preparing and serving the meal and making people feel comfortable. Lazarus sat at the table, and I can imagine every eye went back and forth from him to Jesus. "Then Mary took about a pint of pure nard, an expensive perfume; she poured it on Jesus' feet and wiped his feet with her hair. And the house was filled with the fragrance of the perfume" (John 12:3).

Mary's heart was so full of gratitude and love for Jesus that she couldn't just sit there. She probably asked herself, "What do I have that I can give to the Man who saved my brother? What would be the most extravagant gift I can give Him? I have to do something!" She remembered that in her hope chest was an alabaster jar of the finest perfume. She may have been saving it as part of her dowry in case she got married, but that didn't matter anymore. She went to the other room to get it. When she came back to the party, she looked at Jesus and Lazarus. Only days before, her brother had been dead and decaying in a tomb outside town, but now he sat at a table, talking and laughing with Jesus. Her heart soared with love for Jesus.

She opened the bottle, poured it on His feet, and then used her long hair to gently wipe His feet. Judas complained that she was wasting resources they could have used (and he could have stolen), but Jesus defended her by saying, "Leave her alone....It was intended that she should save this perfume for the day of my burial. You will always have the poor among you, but you will not always have me" (vv. 7–8).

This was a man's world. Women were supposed to stay in the background, but Mary couldn't do that. Just as Jesus had broken barriers to love misfits and outcasts, Mary broke gender and social barriers to pour her love on Jesus.

A few days before, when Jesus had delayed and her brother died, Mary was deeply distressed. Still, when Jesus appeared, she had a glimmer of hope. Following Jesus isn't easy. It's the most challenging adventure life offers, but having Him as Lord of our lives provides more thrills, surprises, and joy than we can imagine.

CHOOSE LOVE

Love is the language of the kingdom, and it's the fuel to expand the kingdom. Love is such a rare commodity in our world that it stands out. If we say we follow Jesus but we aren't learning to love like Him, we're fooling ourselves. When we talk to (or about) addicts, gays, immigrants, gun advocates, people who watch Fox and those who watch MSNBC, those who value masks and social distancing, people on either side of racial justice, and people on the other side of whatever public policy we hold dear, it's perfectly fine to have disagreements about issues, but we shouldn't spew hate.

Jesus had fierce enemies, but we never see Him mock them. He never treated anyone with contempt. Even when He pointed out the sins of the religious leaders, He was inviting them to repent, experience God's love, and walk in kindness and generosity. Jesus doesn't present arguments; He presents Himself. He doesn't bring academic answers to our questions; He's the answer.

> Love is such a rare commodity in our world that it stands out.

We can choose to be self-righteous and resentful. We can choose to stay in our corner and avoid people who disagree with us. Or we can choose to follow Jesus and treat every person with respect. Elizabeth and I are especially concerned about the way people talk about immigrants. The suspicion, wrong assumptions, and hatred are so strong and so wrong. Yes, we need border security, and yes, we need competent ways to screen those who apply for asylum or a green card. But we don't need to use extreme language of exclusion about them. They're people, just like you and me.

Many of them want to escape violence, while others are

seeking better jobs so they can provide for their families. Can't we understand these motivations? Can't we affirm them as human beings as they seek a better life? We can't take in all of them, and we definitely need to screen out those who have committed crimes—but that's a very, very small percentage of the people. Let's treat people who want to come to our country and those who are already here like they're incredibly valuable... because they are.

Follow Jesus. Love the people He loves—which is everybody. Sacrifice a little of your time, and swallow at least some of your presuppositions about people whom you're not drawn to or who are different than you. Remember that they're created in the image of God. Many Christians assume that if they have a respectful conversation with a gay person, they're validating the person's lifestyle. Or if they talk to an undocumented immigrant, they're saying that breaking the law is justified. That's not true at all. Jesus didn't look for reasons to avoid connecting with people. He had one reason to move toward them, no matter who they were or what they'd done: He loved them. Now, His word to us is plain: go and do the same.

DISCUSSION QUESTIONS

- When you think about the scenes of Jesus reaching out to care for people others considered to be undesirable and repugnant, which moments stand out to you? Explain your answer.

- When Jesus touched and healed the leper, how do you think the other lepers felt at that moment? How do you imagine the religious leaders responded?

- Look at Ephesians 4:31–5:2. How does Paul explain the heart of love?

- Paul's warning in 1 Corinthians 13:1–3 was firm and clear. What are some reasons we value gifts, leadership, and sacrifice more than love? How do these misplaced values affect us?

- As you put yourself in the scene of Mary anointing Jesus' feet with expensive perfume, do you think Mary was right to be extravagant? Why or why not?

- If sacrificial, persistent, tenderhearted love is the mark of a true Christian, how do you think most Christians are doing? How about you?

ACTION POINT: WHAT LOVE LOOKS LIKE

Have one conversation with an immigrant this week. Ask why the person has come to America, and ask what challenges he or she faces.

CHAPTER 6

CONFRONT YOUR INNER PHARISEE

For many readers, I'm sure the title of this chapter is hard to swallow. Keep reading anyway. This is important.

One time, I was asked to attend a meeting with prominent pastors in the Chicago area. One of the pastors asked for our input on a problem he was having. It seems that a number of undocumented immigrants had started attending his church, and his board didn't want to extend membership to them. He asked us, "What should we do with this problem?"

I couldn't believe he would even pose such a question. "Problem?" I responded. "What's the problem with them joining your church?"

The pastor was surprised by my question. He replied a bit defensively, "Well, they're not legally in this country."

My anger was rising, and I didn't miss a beat. "Pastor, are you taking their offerings?"

"Uh, yes, we are."

I paused for a second to make sure I wanted to say what was on my heart, and then I spoke up: "My friend, it's hypocritical to take their money but not their names." As he was thinking about my comment, I told him, "Hey, send them to our church. We have no problem taking their names and their money!"

By that time, I had been to a meatpacking plant in Postville, Iowa, where in 2008 almost four hundred undocumented immigrants were rounded up and 297 served five months in jail before they were shipped back to their countries.[1] I was outraged at their treatment—not that they were held accountable but that they were treated like cattle. When the Pharisees stood around Jesus as He enjoyed time with the prostitutes and tax collectors in Luke 15, they had two distinct classifications of people: acceptable and unacceptable. Jesus had only one category: loved.

In one of the meetings of pastors in Chicago and White House staff members to talk about the problems of the inner city, one of the president's staff members asked us, "What's the problem with Chicago?"

They assumed someone would talk about gun violence, gangs, drugs, or the lack of economic opportunities, but I answered, "It's the church."

Every eye turned to me. "Christians have become so politicized that we've lost our ability to be salt and light. We're no longer a city on a hill shining brightly for everyone to see. We're no different from the other angry people who caricature those who disagree with them, and it's killing our witness. Churches are in every neighborhood, but we're just taking up space. We're failing at our primary responsibility to represent the love of Jesus to a broken and desperate world."

A MOMENT IN PROTOCOL

A few years ago, I was invited to meet with the king of Burkina Faso in Africa. I was given instructions that outlined the protocol for people who meet with him. I was instructed how to enter the presence of the king, where to stand, how to sit, how to speak, and how to leave the room. I listened intently because I didn't want any drama—and I wanted to make sure I got back home! But mostly, I wanted to honor the king.

Christians in our country have two protocols: secular and spiritual. The American secular directives are to get everything you can and pursue financial security, fame, and fun. Another set of secular instructions is to live for a political ideology, one that champions the values and rights you hold dear. Many Christians in America are fiercely dedicated to both parts of the secular protocol.

The protocol of the kingdom of heaven is quite the opposite: consider others as more important than yourself, give sacrificially and generously, lose your life to find it, and be a good ambassador to the people of the other kingdom.

The Pharisees had all the outward trappings of living by a kingdom protocol, but closer inspection shows that they were far more committed to their own power and prestige than to the kingdom Jesus was inaugurating. We saw Jesus reach out to them in His parable of the prodigal son, inviting them to join Him and the repentant sinners at the feast of salvation, but they ridiculed Him instead. In a series of statements in Matthew's Gospel, Jesus held a mirror in front of them and showed them how far they were from the heart of God. Seven times, Jesus called them hypocrites because they claimed godliness but practiced selfishness. For instance, He told them:

> You give a tenth of your spices—mint, dill and cumin. But you have neglected the more important matters of the law—justice, mercy and faithfulness. You should have practiced the latter, without neglecting the former. You blind guides! You strain out a gnat but swallow a camel.... You are like whitewashed tombs, which look beautiful on the outside but on the inside are full of the bones of the dead and everything unclean. In the same way, on the outside you appear to people as righteous but on the inside you are full of hypocrisy and wickedness.
>
> —MATTHEW 23:23–24, 27–28

Perhaps the clearest description of how the Pharisees missed the heart of God was in Jesus' quote from the Old Testament when He spoke to them: "These people honor me with their lips, but their hearts are far from me" (Matt. 15:8).

Jesus' kingdom has protocols that the Pharisees weren't willing to follow. It would have required them to turn their lives upside down, and that was a bridge too far. They couldn't conceive of letting go of their prominent place in society and letting God transform their hearts so they lived with "justice, mercy, and faithfulness."

We usually think of justice as punishing the guilty, but in the Old Testament, the primary meaning was caring for the poor. That's why the poor rejoiced when the judge appeared (Ps. 75:7–10; 96:13; and others)—he would right the wrongs of oppression. Mercy is meeting the needs of people, and faithfulness is the persistent commitment to the purposes of God, no matter what others think of us. Clearly, the

Pharisees looked like the strongest supporters of God's cause in their day, but Jesus showed that they completely missed God's heart. They were very religious but for radically wrong reasons. They were trying to establish a kingdom where they called the shots.

When Jesus stood before the Roman governor Pilate, He told him, "My kingdom is not of this world" (John 18:36). The same is true for all of us who claim Him as our Savior. Our true home is God's kingdom where God rules and where we honor Him and His values over everything else.

Getting back to my meeting with the king of Burkina Faso, I informed him that I'm an ambassador of the kingdom of heaven and I represent the King of kings and Lord of lords—the same thing I tell the people at our church. I'm an American, but my higher allegiance is to God. His kingdom has a different currency, a different language, a different purpose, different values, and a different culture.

I'm afraid that many, even most, of the Christians in our country are more loyal to the American dream or a political party than to Jesus. I'm not trying to be harsh, just honest. The Pharisees were just like that. They had their hands on power, and they held onto it with a death grip even as the Son of Man offered His love and grace to them. They wanted power and prestige more than following Him, and I fear that many believers in America have made the same calculation and arrived at the same answer.

When we follow Jesus, we drop the Republican flag, the Democratic flag, the rainbow flag, the gun rights flag, the Puerto Rican flag, and even the American flag. Yes, I love America. I was born here, and I'm deeply grateful for the wonderful opportunities living in this country has given me.

But I love Jesus more. I may delight in Puerto Rican history, food, and music, but I delight in the grace of Jesus Christ far more.

I know that some of you are thinking, "I knew it! Choco is a flaming liberal, another Hispanic who doesn't love our country." I assure you that's not true. And some want to scream, "But America is a Christian nation! Can't we honor it that way?"

The history of the founding of America is much more complicated than that. Some of the signers of the Declaration of Independence and the Constitution were Christians, but most were deists and not Bible-believing, salvation-by-faith Christians. And the country was begun with a devil's bargain to allow slavery,[2] a decision that led to the carnage that ripped the country apart less than ninety years later.

I can hear it now: "Choco doesn't believe in American exceptionalism." Actually I believe this is a truly exceptional country, but this land is not without its flaws...and flawed leaders. People and history are much more interesting than two-dimensional representations of our heritage.

Why do I make these points in this book? Because many of us are more loyal to America (or, more accurately, our particular vision of America) than to God. We are more passionate about politics than missions and more discouraged when our political party loses than when the gospel doesn't reach various segments of society.

I believe part of the problem is that God has blessed this country so much that we expect unending prosperity and peace in this life. Our hope is set on the temporal, not the eternal. We need to remember that "our citizenship is in heaven" (Phil. 3:20).

RIGHT BUT WRONG

It's not enough to pride ourselves in being the righteous people (as in, "I'm not like those people") and holding the right convictions about the things that are most important. Being right isn't the same thing as loving. The Pharisees were considered the good guys in first-century Palestine because they upheld the traditions and honored the Scriptures in the face of Roman occupation and widespread discouragement. They were dedicated to what was right, and they condemned people who didn't follow their path. The people were in awe of them and feared the leaders.

In His most famous sermon, Jesus undoubtedly shocked the people listening to Him when He said, "For I tell you, unless your righteousness exceeds that of the scribes and Pharisees, you will never enter the kingdom of heaven" (Matt. 5:20, ESV). Exceed them? They were so perfect in their obedience that they added hundreds of extra rules to be sure they didn't break any of God's rules! But

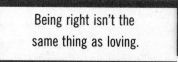

Being right isn't the same thing as loving.

Jesus wasn't equating righteousness with keeping rigid rules. He was talking about having a sensitive heart toward God, loving Him supremely, and obeying out of gratitude instead of fear. This kind of righteousness loves the unlovely and is appropriately angry about injustice inflicted on the powerless.

Before we bought the farm outside Chicago, we purchased a building in our neighborhood and raised $50,000 to renovate it. After a few months, the property was ready. At a church board meeting, I proposed that we use the building as a shelter for homeless women. One of the deacons was furious, however. "Why in the world would we waste this new building and all this money on people who will make it filthy?" he asked. "They won't take care of the place. In a few weeks, we'll have to replace everything. It doesn't make sense!"

I completely understood his point of view, but I didn't back down. For years, every dime and every moment of our time were devoted to the people and programs within the walls of the church. Reaching outside our walls was new to all of us, and it was hard for this man to get his head around it.

The painful question for each of us is, Who are the insiders who deserve my love, and who are the outsiders who don't? Jesus had this conversation with a religious leader who wanted to make Jesus look foolish.

> "Teacher," [the expert in the law] asked, "what must I do to inherit eternal life?"
>
> "What is written in the Law?" he replied. "How do you read it?"
>
> He answered, "'Love the Lord your God with all your heart and with all your soul and with all your strength and with all your mind'; and, 'Love your neighbor as yourself.'"
>
> "You have answered correctly," Jesus replied. "Do this and you will live."
>
> But he wanted to justify himself, so he asked Jesus, "And who is my neighbor?"
>
> —LUKE 10:25–29

Jesus was ready with a powerful and beautiful answer to the man's question. He told a parable about a Jewish man who was going to Jericho, maybe on business. This road was sometimes called "the bloody road" because thugs were so common. On the way, this Jewish man was attacked, beaten, stripped, and robbed, "leaving him half dead" (v. 30). The man was in a desperate condition, and he needed help right away.

A priest, who may have just finished serving in the temple, walked up and saw the man's condition. We don't know how many sacrifices the priest performed that day or what prayers he offered, but nothing moved him to care for the man. He realized that touching the man's blood would make him ceremonially unclean. He may have calculated that the time to go back to Jerusalem to go through ritual cleansing would cost him too much time, so he walked on by.

Then a Levite, who helped the priests at the temple, walked down the road and past the man. He may have sung one of the psalms about the mercy of God. But when he saw the man on the side of the road, he considered the cost of stopping to help, and he walked past him. The two men who represented God to the people of God didn't have the heart of God to care for a man in trouble. Then, a Samaritan saw the bleeding and broken man on the side of the road. Jesus tells us about his heart and character.

> He took pity on him. He went to him and bandaged his wounds, pouring on oil and wine. Then he put the man on his own donkey, brought him to an inn and took care of him. The next day he took out two denarii and gave them to the innkeeper. "Look after him," he said, "and when I return, I will reimburse you for any extra expense you may have."
>
> —LUKE 10:33–35

Remember that the Jews viewed the Samaritans as half-breeds and hated them, yet Jesus makes a Samaritan the hero of the story. And oh, what a hero! He tended to the man's wounds, let him ride on his donkey, gave him shelter and personal attention, and then paid for the man's care, including an open-ended expense account for anything else he might need. He didn't worry that touching the man might make him ceremonially unclean, and he didn't run past him because he worried that the thugs were waiting to ambush anyone who stopped to help.

It's important to note that the Samaritan didn't screen the man's background to see if he was worthy of his help. He didn't ask others to find out whether the man's problems were his own fault. He didn't have categories of people who deserved his care and those who didn't. He just responded to the obvious need with kindness and generosity.

After telling this story and letting it sink in, Jesus turned to the religious leader.

> "Which of these three do you think was a neighbor to the man who fell into the hands of robbers?"
> The expert in the law replied, "The one who had mercy on him."
> Jesus told him, "Go and do likewise."
> —LUKE 10:36–37

The religious leader was so prejudiced that he wouldn't even say the word *Samaritan*. He grudgingly admitted that only the despised foreigner represented the heart of God. Jesus must have smiled when He told him, in effect, "Be the guy you despise, not the one you honor."

The Pharisees were more loyal to the Law and their additions to the Law than they were to the Lord. They insisted that they were right and that they held the banner of righteousness. The religious leaders positioned themselves to be seen as the noblest and godliest people in their society, but Jesus said they were hypocrites. His gentle, tenacious love for people stood in stark contrast to the poverty of the Pharisees' hearts.

WHO ARE WE?

Jesus' parables invite us to ask, "Who am I in the story?" At some point, all of us have been the man on the side of the road. We were broken by the circumstances of life, beaten and bloody, and left hopeless and abandoned. Others may have seen us and passed by or, worse, stopped to condemn us. We felt alone, heartbroken, and empty. We had nothing to offer God, but Jesus stopped to care for us, heal our wounds, and give us a new start.

It would be instructive to take a hard look at the two men who passed by. They found excuses to avoid getting involved in the man's predicament, deeming the situation too messy and inconvenient for them to stop to help. I believe all of us have the tendency to be Pharisees, especially those who have been in church for years. We wear a mask that says we have it all together, but we hide the fact that our motives are tainted by superiority and selfishness. Like the priest and the Levite, we do plenty of good things, and we have plenty of excuses to avoid getting involved in the messiness sur-rounding the lives of the poor; alcoholics, addicts, and their families; parents of struggling adolescents; couples who live in constant tension without real affection; victims of abuse; and people with mental illness, chronic depression, and a host of other sticky, disorderly problems.

But that's precisely what Jesus did for us. Was it inconvenient for Him to step out of the glory of heaven to take the role of a humble servant among us? Was it costly for Him to love us so much that He suffered humiliation, attacks by enemies, abandonment by friends, and the shameful, cruel death by Roman crucifixion?

We get a glimpse of the cost when we look at Him in the Garden of Gethsemane before Judas brought the soldiers to arrest Him. He asked Peter, James, and John, his closest friends on earth, to be with Him. He told them, "'My soul is overwhelmed with sorrow to the point of death. Stay here and keep watch with me.' Going a little farther, he fell with his face to the ground and prayed, 'My Father, if it is possible, may this cup be taken from me. Yet not as I will, but as you will'" (Matt. 26:38–39).

In the garden, Jesus looked into the abyss of hell—the hell each of us deserves and the hell He endured in our place. Still, He loved you and me so much that He resolved to endure physical torture and the excruciating pain of being separated from the Father.

That night, Jesus was betrayed, arrested, and found guilty in an unlawful trial. A few hours later, in the morning, He was taken before the Roman governor, who wanted to free Him, but the crowds who had cheered Him the week before now called for His death. He was brutally whipped, taken to a hill outside the city gates, and nailed to a cross, and He died an excruciating death. At any point, Jesus could have walked away and saved Himself all the agony.

At His arrest, when Peter used a sword to try to defend Him, Jesus asked His misguided friend, "Do you think I cannot call on my Father, and he will at once put at my disposal twelve legions of angels?" (Matt. 26:53). It was within

His power to stop what was happening to Him at any time. Pastor Tim Keller quotes Charles Spurgeon, saying,

> Jesus Christ was up on the cross…looking down on the people betraying him, and forsaking him, and denying him, and in the greatest act of love in the history of the universe, he stayed![3]

Are you moved by the cross of Jesus? Does His love displayed with His arms nailed wide melt your heart, galvanize your purpose, and compel you to live and love like He did?

When we encounter the crucified and risen Christ, He lives in us and transforms us from the inside out. We love the unlovely because Jesus loved us when we were dead and hopeless. We forgive those who have hurt us because Jesus paid the price to forgive us and we have a deep well to draw from. And we accept people who are different from us because Jesus accepted us as His friends and brothers and sisters when we had nothing to offer Him. He is the true elder brother who moved heaven and earth to find us and bring us home.[4]

The meaning of the gospel doesn't end the moment after we trust Christ. It's just the beginning! The sacrifice of Christ continues to mold us, correct us, inspire us, and energize us to live for Him instead of ourselves. Far too many Christians have compartmentalized their faith into ninety minutes on a Sunday morning and seldom think about God the rest of the week. If they attend church, they check off the spirituality box, and they're done until the next Sunday. Instead, the love of Jesus should permeate every moment of every day, in our relationships with our spouse and children, our talk about current events, our relationships at work, our leisure time, and our interactions with friends. Jesus is Lord all the time! And He has called us to let love be our aim all the time.

Jesus didn't die only for those who mean well but fall a little short. The gospel isn't for pretty good people who need a bit of help to be more acceptable. Jesus sees us for who we are: totally lost, without hope, enemies of God, and spiritually dead, with nothing that can impress Him so He'll accept us. But He loves us still.

To the extent we experience this amazing love, we'll lay down our pencil and checklist of criteria about who deserves our help and who doesn't. Yes, the person who drinks too much has caused his own problems, the woman on the street made some bad choices, the teenager who rebels against his parents is on a self-destructive path, but none of them is beyond the love of God. He wants to bless these people— and the hands He uses are ours, the feet He uses are ours, and the voices He uses are ours. It's not our job to categorize people as deserving or undeserving. It's our job to love.

We're not on our own as we try to love like Jesus. The Holy Spirit lives within us, and His role is to convict us when we're drifting (or running) away from God's purposes, instruct us in the way to go, give us specific direction to respond to needs, and empower us to make a difference in the lives of others. In salvation, it's all God's work to bring us to Himself. All we have to do is say yes to Him.

But in our spiritual growth, our sanctification, we play a part by obeying. We're partners with the Holy Spirit in our own growth and our impact on others. Paul described this in his letter to the Philippians: "Therefore, my dear friends, as you have always obeyed—not only in my presence, but now much more in my absence—continue to work out your salvation with fear and trembling, for it is God who works in you to will and to act in order to fulfill his good purpose" (2:12–13).

We don't work for our salvation, but we work out our salvation in response to the greatness and grace of God, which, if we grasp the wonder of who He is, produces godly fear (reverence) and trembling (wonder). Any impact we have, any change we see in ourselves, is the result of our obedience and the Holy Spirit's power unleashed in and through us.

I like to think of a car as an analogy of how the Holy Spirit works in us. The Spirit is our GPS to show us the way and the

> It's not our job to categorize people as deserving or undeserving. It's our job to love.

engine that propels us there. Our part is to get in the car, stay in the car, and respond to the Spirit's directions so we get where He wants us to go. If we stay in touch with the Holy Spirit, the love of God becomes a power that changes lives—first ours and then those around us.

As I listen to many Christians today, it seems that too many are living in fear. They believe they're losing the battle, and they're upset with anyone who threatens to undermine their security. Fear paralyzes, fear divides, and fear inflames suspicion about others. But "perfect love casts out fear" (1 John 4:18, ESV). Our commitment to "love them anyway" addresses these fears and asks the question, "What do we do now in this climate of suspicion and hate, in this polarized culture?"

The Pharisees were afraid of losing their lofty position and power. They struggled to maintain their exalted status in the middle of the Roman occupation, and they became narrow, defensive, and proud. They believed they were the heroes of the nation. They trusted in their virtues instead of trusting in God. Are a lot of Christians in our country like them, at least in some ways? Am I? Are you?

> Fear paralyzes, fear divides, and fear inflames suspicion about others. But "perfect love casts out fear" (1 John 4:18, ESV).

We can ask God to overwhelm us with His love so that we're more like Jesus than the Pharisees. I love this prayer found in Paul's letter to the Ephesians:

> For this reason I kneel before the Father, from whom every family in heaven and on earth derives its name. I pray that out of his glorious riches he may strengthen you with power through his Spirit in your inner being, so that Christ may dwell in your hearts through faith. And I pray that you, being rooted and established in love, may have power, together with all the Lord's holy people, to grasp how wide and long and high and deep is the love of Christ, and to know this love that surpasses knowledge—that you may be filled to the measure of all the fullness of God.
>
> Now to him who is able to do immeasurably more than all we ask or imagine, according to his power that is at work within us, to him be glory in the church and in Christ Jesus throughout all generations, for ever and ever! Amen.
>
> —Ephesians 3:14–21

A transformed heart doesn't happen without both the power and the love of God. Do you feel more comfortable as a Pharisee? I hope not. No matter where you are in your journey, pray this prayer and expect God to answer it.

DISCUSSION QUESTIONS

- It's not pleasant or comfortable to consider if (and to what degree) we're like the Pharisees. What were their strengths during the Roman occupation? In what ways did they fail miserably?

- How would you distinguish between the protocol of the American dream and the protocol of God's kingdom?

- Do you agree or disagree with the concept that we need to raise the Christian flag in our hearts higher than the American flag (or the flag of a political party or cause)? Explain your answer.

- Read Luke 10:25–37. What "good excuses" did the priest and the Levite probably tell themselves as they walked past the man on the road to Jericho? How do you see similar excuses used by people who stand back and criticize people who are struggling (such as addicts, immigrants, etc.)?

- Who are the people in your world bleeding on the side of the road?

- Who are you in the parable? Explain your answer.

- Whom do you know whose heart has truly been melted by a deep grasp of the wonder of the cross? Is that person's life attractive to you? Why or why not?

ACTION POINT: WHAT LOVE LOOKS LIKE

Take time to read, study, and paraphrase Paul's prayer in Ephesians 3. Write a paragraph about what it will look like when love compels you to be like the good Samaritan.

CHAPTER 7

BEYOND TOLERANCE

IN 2009, CITY officials considered appointing me as an alderman—a fancy title given to members of Chicago's City Council. The man who put my name forward had served in the position for sixteen years. He planned to serve the first two years of his term, and I would serve the remaining two years before the next election.

Traditionally, the mayor rubber-stamps approval for the person the retiring alderman recommends, so things looked good for me to be appointed. When word got out in Humboldt Park, however, the reaction was decidedly mixed. While a number of people were excited about the possibility that I would represent them, the LGBTQ community was outraged. They spread gossip that I was homophobic and there was no way I could represent them, and they dug up a laundry list of accusations and condemnations to strengthen their stand.

Members of the gay and lesbian community had started a number of organizations in our neighborhood, and someone suggested that I invite them to a meeting. I reserved a private room in the back of a restaurant for an evening and invited the leaders of the organizations to join me. They came, and they also brought many of their members.

The room was packed when I walked in alone. I didn't take anyone with me. One of the ladies who led one of the organizations made the introductions. She asked me to tell a little bit about myself, so I explained that I'm a product of the community and that I've lived through some turbulent times. I added that I went to the school just down the street, and I told them about my family. Then I said, "I'm here to answer any questions and address any concerns you have about me possibly becoming a city alderman. The floor is open."

For the next hour, people asked questions, but some chose to make insulting comments instead of asking a question. Several of their statements were similar: "You Christians say you're all about love, but you don't want us to love the people we want to love. That's hypocritical! That's not fair!" They wanted to see how I'd respond. I thanked each one for his or her input and moved on.

In the middle of the hour, someone asked, "Would you be willing to change what's on your church's website about homosexuality?"

Our website addresses issues of theology, community, and opportunities to serve, and one of our statements is that homosexuality isn't God's design for marriage—in fact it's a sin. I knew exactly what the person was asking. "No, we aren't going to change the website," I responded.

Another person quickly asked, "Well, then, are you willing to make a public statement that you accept the freedom for people to choose a homosexual lifestyle?"

"I'm not sure I understand the question," I answered. "Everybody knows I don't accept the homosexual lifestyle, so it's already public."

I was in the hot seat. Most of the people in the room glared at me in anger. They certainly didn't want to hear me disagree with their principles and choices. I was standing alone, but I knew I wasn't alone. Person after person tried to make me waver in my convictions or trick me to say something I didn't mean, but the Lord gave me a calm spirit and a clear mind.

At the end of the meeting, I told them plainly but without raising my voice, "For thirty years, you have fought for tolerance. You've insisted that people accept your lifestyle as equally valid as traditional marriage, but tonight, you've been intolerant of me and my faith. You've called me a hypocrite, but tonight, you've been hypocritical."

The room was dead silent, and then a lady stood up and told the group, "I may disagree with the reverend, but tonight he came to listen and answer our questions. I'm going to support his candidacy." Several others stood up and said something similar. It took guts for them to speak up for me in that hostile environment.[1]

That night, the people in the room felt conflicted. I was one of them, from the same neighborhood and with the same history, but I wasn't one of them in my beliefs and values. Our church serves the poor, including a lot of gays, lesbians, and transgender people, so they knew I didn't hate them. But they couldn't accept my faith. They wanted me to change, or at least to soften my convictions, but I couldn't do that. In the meeting, I showed them the love of Jesus simply by showing up and being courteous to them. I didn't bark back when they accused me of being intolerant, and I didn't demand that they agree with my positions. I didn't hold up a sign that said, "You're going to hell!" I treated them with respect, even when they didn't reciprocate. I spoke my truth without anger and without wavering, and God used me to build some bridges with at least a few people there.

Reuben, one of the men at the restaurant that night, was known throughout the community as a flamboyant gay. He was a big guy, very vocal, as well as imposing, loud, and hostile. I saw him from time to time around the neighborhood.

Three years after that meeting in the restaurant, one of my staff members called and said, "A man named Reuben wants to meet with you." I tried to think of every person in our church or our neighborhood named Reuben, but no one came to mind. Still, I agreed to see him. I set up an appointment at our church-sponsored café. When I arrived, I instantly remembered meeting him years before, but this time, he had changed his wardrobe from wild colors to a gray suit. I gave him a hug and said, "I heard that you want to meet with me."

He smiled. "Yes, thanks for coming, Pastor."

We sat down, and I asked, "What's going on? How can I help?"

He took a deep breath. "Pastor, I've had an encounter with the Lord, and He has changed my life. I'm moving out of Humboldt Park and going to Florida to get away from all my gay friends. I need a place where I can focus on my relationship with Jesus. The Lord told me that before I leave, I need to reconcile with you. That's why I called."

"Thank you," I said, leaning in to hear more.

He took a deep breath and continued. "I said a lot of things about you that weren't true."

I nodded and noticed that he was crying, actually sobbing. Through his tears, he told me, "Pastor, I need to ask you to forgive me."

I leaned over and put my arm around him. "Brother, I forgave you three years ago. That very night. There's nothing wrong between us. You're my brother in the Lord now. That's what matters."

A day or two later, he moved to Florida. Over the years, I've heard that he's doing well, walking with God and serving Him. What happened is a beautiful result of the tense meeting in our neighborhood.

GRACE *AND* TRUTH

The traditional definition of *tolerance* is sympathy for others' beliefs that conflict with our own, even admitting that our views may be wrong. But today's definition refuses to assess right and wrong, assuming that all beliefs, values, and lifestyles are equally valid.

As an example, the old definition of *tolerance* is rooted in the belief that there is objective truth, but the new one says, "I have my truth, you have your truth, and they're equally acceptable." Today, if you voice even a mild disagreement with someone's concept of truth, you'll be criticized for being intolerant. People will accuse you of not being loving, lacking grace, and being hateful. That's a very small box you have to fit into!

John tells us that Jesus came "full of grace and truth" (John 1:14), not one or the other. Grace and truth must go together, like peanut butter and jelly, Batman and Robin, or the Lone

Ranger and Tonto. Grace without truth is only emotion, and truth without grace is the legalism of harsh demands and guilt motivation.

One of the most common statements made today is a quote from the Sermon on the Mount: "Don't judge!" We hear people say it whenever anyone voices a criticism or even an opinion. To understand this short but powerful statement, we need to look at the context of the passage.

> Do not judge, or you too will be judged. For in the same way you judge others, you will be judged, and with the measure you use, it will be measured to you.
> —MATTHEW 7:1–2

The word *judge* has a range of meaning. You might say, "I cut the board too short because I didn't judge the length accurately." In that context, the word simply means an observation without a value judgment. But if you say, "I was asked to judge the best tomatoes at the county fair," then this is an assessment with a value judgment, albeit without condemnation.

In other words, Jesus isn't saying that we can't make assessments and we can't differentiate right from wrong or good from bad—He did that all the time! And the Bible is full of these judgments. In fact, later in this passage, Jesus calls some people dogs and pigs. I think that's a value judgment! So, what point is Jesus making? He wants us to avoid delighting in finding fault in others or harshly condemning them while feeling superior. It's not wrong to simply state the facts—that's observation. So, read this carefully: you harshly judge when you assume to know the motives of people's hearts and when you conclude that you're better than they are.

To illustrate this concept, Jesus uses a metaphor that you might find comical, but He uses exaggerations for a purpose.

> Why do you look at the speck of sawdust in your brother's eye and pay no attention to the plank in your own eye? How can you say to your brother, "Let me take the speck out of your eye," when all the time there is a plank in your own eye? You hypocrite, first take the plank out of your own eye, and then you will see clearly to remove the speck from your brother's eye.
>
> —MATTHEW 7:3–5

The plank and the speck are character flaws. Our normal tendency is to see others' flaws as huge boards, but we think ours are only tiny specks. Yet Jesus reverses this perception. If we believe we're superior or better than, the sin of pride blinds us so that we can't see anything clearly. We may want to focus on the flaw in the other person, but our first priority should be to look in the mirror and deal with our arrogance, our wrong perception, and our blindness. Then, we'll have the humility and perception to gently, carefully help the person overcome a character flaw.

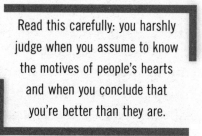

Read this carefully: you harshly judge when you assume to know the motives of people's hearts and when you conclude that you're better than they are.

This illustration isn't just a theory; we need to apply it in every relationship. When you're dating, you don't see specks or planks in your girlfriend or boyfriend, but after a few years of marriage, many couples have collected enough insults and hurts that they've built up a case against each other. They have enough planks to build a mansion!

We can also build a case for the prosecution against people at work (especially employers), against friends and neighbors, and against people in the church. The statement that should stop us in our tracks is in verse 2: "For in the same way you judge others, you will be judged, and with the measure you use, it will be measured to you."

If you're harsh, others will be harsh toward you. If you make a habit of finding everything wrong with another person, that person will look for your flaws too. This is simply the way human nature works, but it can be reversed. Keep in mind what Jesus said a few verses later: "So in everything, do to others what you would have them do to you, for this sums up the Law and the Prophets" (v. 12).

We can draw a distinction between a critical judgment and a charitable judgment. A critical judgment mocks, "I'll destroy you!" But a charitable judgment sees the same flaws and asks, "How can I help you?" One is motivated by superiority and resentment; the other is propelled by love.

Sometimes, we're critical because we don't have the facts, and when we have the wrong facts, we inevitably draw the wrong conclusions. I heard a story about a pastor who sat in his car in the parking lot on a Sunday morning reviewing his sermon notes before the service. He was using a white pencil, and as he read, he absentmindedly held it in his mouth. One of the deacons walked by and saw him with the white pencil jutting out from his lips. He ran inside and gathered as many deacons as he could find. When the pastor came in, the group confronted him for smoking in the parking lot. The pastor smiled, pulled his pencil out of his pocket, and put it in his mouth.

Even if we have the facts—even if we're eyewitnesses—we

can be wrong. We're human, our perception is limited, and we come to every conversation and every event with our own presuppositions based on past experiences.

The Battle of Gettysburg was a turning point in the American Civil War. The armies of North and South fought for three crucial days until the Southern army finally retreated. Four months later, President Abraham Lincoln dedicated the cemetery on the site of the battle in a three-minute speech. His address was so short that many people hadn't settled into their

> We can draw a distinction between a critical judgment and a charitable judgment.... One is motivated by superiority and resentment; the other is propelled by love.

seats before he finished. Some journalists at the time criticized Lincoln's Gettysburg address as "silly" and shameful and said it should be forgotten.[2] But within a generation, what Lincoln said on the battlefield was considered perhaps the finest speech ever delivered by an American president.

TRUTH IN LOVE

It's our God-given responsibility to be observant and form objective opinions of events, organizations, and people. How best to do that? By opening our eyes and seeing the impact of our actions.

Plenty of people say the right things, but their lives aren't consistent with their words. In the same passage in His sermon, Jesus warned about people like this.

> Watch out for false prophets. They come to you in sheep's clothing, but inwardly they are ferocious wolves. By their fruit you will recognize them. Do people

pick grapes from thornbushes, or figs from thistles? Likewise, every good tree bears good fruit, but a bad tree bears bad fruit. A good tree cannot bear bad fruit, and a bad tree cannot bear good fruit. Every tree that does not bear good fruit is cut down and thrown into the fire. Thus, by their fruit you will recognize them.

—MATTHEW 7:15–20

When I go to the grocery store to buy fruits and vegetables, I inspect them very carefully. Elizabeth always has me pick out the avocados because I really enjoy eating them, and they need to be just right. When I go to choose avocados, some of them aren't quite ripe, others are beyond the best stage, and a few are just right.

That's how Jesus wants us to observe people around us. Most of the people in our churches need to mature a bit more before they're ripe. That doesn't mean we reject them; it means we encourage them and give them time to grow. We don't condemn them for where they are, and we don't leave them for where they are.

In Paul's letter to the Ephesians, he observes that we need each other in order to grow strong in our faith. Today, many people assume they can walk with God in power and intimacy on their own, but that would be news to Paul, who told us that when we are in close relationships, we'll grow in faith and knowledge:

Then we will no longer be infants, tossed back and forth by the waves, and blown here and there by every wind of teaching and by the cunning and craftiness of people in their deceitful scheming. Instead, speaking the truth in love, we will grow to become in every respect the mature body of him who is the head, that is, Christ. From him the whole body, joined and held together by every supporting ligament, grows and builds itself up in love, as each part does its work.

—EPHESIANS 4:14–16

The central element of these relationships is our ability to speak the truth in love. When we don't, people aren't encouraged, convicted, challenged, or inspired. When we have the courage and compassion—it takes both—to move into people's lives and love them enough to be honest, amazing things can happen. How can we speak this way? Let me offer some suggestions:

- Focus on the positives. Yes, that person is annoying. Yes, he or she does things that are far worse than annoying. But if all we talk about are the faults and flaws, we create an adversarial relationship. We build bridges by drawing attention to the positive qualities and things people do right.

- Don't insist on being right. When winning is your primary goal, you look for every opportunity to defeat the other person. These relationships are a zero-sum game: there's a winner and a loser, and you're determined to avoid losing!

- Disagree agreeably. Even the best of friends disagree from time to time, and in some relationships, the value divide is a canyon. Your goal is understanding, not dominance. When you redefine winning, you'll ask good questions,

listen carefully, and walk away as friends. One
of the signs that you're seeking understanding
is making the simple request, "Tell me more
about that." It works wonders.

- Watch your body language. People can tell
what you really think and feel by noticing how
you stand or sit, how your arms are crossed
or uncrossed, and how much eye contact you
give—and the look in your eyes when you
make eye contact. In the middle of conversations, do a quick analysis of the message you're
sending with your posture and expression. The
vast majority of the impact of communication
is in body language, gestures, and tone of voice.
The actual words often have a minimal effect.

- Pursue restoration. Far too many of our disagreements are spoken in anger because we're
drawing from the wrong well. Instead of the
deep and refreshing water of Christ's love,
we've been drinking of contempt for those who
have different beliefs.

James, the half-brother of Jesus, ended his letter with this
encouragement:

> My brothers and sisters, if one of you should wander
> from the truth and someone should bring that person
> back, remember this: Whoever turns a sinner from the
> error of their way will save them from death and cover
> over a multitude of sins.
>
> —James 5:19–20

We can make two important assumptions about this directive. First, there are plenty of times when people in the family of God drift off course and need someone to help them get back on the straight path. Second, love is essential to bring them back. Guilt and pressure may work for a short while, but love has far more staying power. This principle applies to our connections with everyone, not just our relationships with believers.

Sometimes we're passive, and the absence of love allows a breeding ground for hate. Scientists say that "nature abhors a vacuum," which means something will always fill up a void. Don't leave a void that can be filled with hate, and don't give the enemy an opportunity to turn small offenses into genuine bitterness. For instance, if there's a misunderstanding or even a cross word with someone, take the initiative to fill up the space with words that bring understanding, peace, and love.

Don't leave the space empty and assume everything will be fine. It won't. Be the peacemaker. Put away your pride and love people enough to move in their direction. Value and honor them. Our natural reaction to offenses is fight, flight, or freeze. Don't do what's natural; do what's supernatural—speak the truth in love, be willing to confront, but be kind. Be strong enough to stay engaged when you want to run away.

We're not the first generation having to grapple with inflammatory, polarizing cultural issues such as gay marriage, abortion rights, climate change, gun rights, and immigration. Jesus had plenty. The Romans occupied the Jewish homeland, and the Jewish people were afraid of losing the culture wars. The Romans demanded taxes, and some fellow Jews collaborated to collect them. Religious leaders created additional laws that were designed to promote purity but in reality were a burden too heavy to bear.

Against this backdrop, people were looking for a Messiah—but one who would be a military hero to kick the Romans out of Palestine and restore Israel to its former glory. In the middle of all this, Jesus focused on the things that really mattered, answered questions with amazing wisdom, and kept loving people even when they

> Don't do what's natural; do what's supernatural—speak the truth in love, be willing to confront, but be kind.

didn't understand His heart or His mission. He didn't merely tolerate people and let them believe whatever they wanted to believe. Instead, He spoke truth, kept speaking truth when others called Him insane and demon-possessed, and ultimately died for the truth, but it was all from a heart of love.

Jesus went far beyond tolerance. He didn't stand back and say, "Hey, you can believe and act any way you choose. Everything's equally valid." He spoke gracious truth to those who would listen, and He spoke hard truth to the obstinate. His purpose for both was the same: to bring them to salvation by grace alone and faith alone.

DISCUSSION QUESTIONS

- When Jesus said, "Don't judge," what did He mean? What didn't He mean? Why is this distinction important?

- When is it wise to walk away from a disagreement? How do you know when you've reached that point in your conversations with people? Explain your answer.

- Read Ephesians 4:14–16. Whom do you know who speaks the truth in love in difficult relationships? What impact does that person have on others?

- How do you know when to challenge someone's values and reason and when to let the issue slide? Are you skilled in knowing the difference? Explain your answer.

- When is it a good idea to pursue restoration? Is it ever unwise or wrong? Explain your answer.

- Do you think it's desirable to be friends with people who disagree with you on important issues? Is it even possible? Why or why not?

ACTION POINT: WHAT LOVE LOOKS LIKE

This week, be a student of your body language. Make a note or set your alarm to remind you three times a day to reflect on what your posture, facial expressions, and tone of voice communicated in previous conversations. How did these differ from the words you spoke?

CHAPTER 8

BUILD BRIDGES

WHERE DO YOU and I draw the line between the people who are messing up their lives but still have value and those we give up on? When my son, Wilfredo Jr., was flunking out of school and smoking marijuana, I never had a thought of giving up on him. Sure, I was upset, frustrated, and deeply disappointed, but his behavior got more of my attention, not less.

But others are harder to love, and it's more difficult to believe they'll ever change. Miriam had a good job and was involved with her daughter Stephanie's school...until her brother offered her a hit of crack cocaine. Like many others, Miriam got hooked quickly, and her life crashed into a deep pit of addiction and selfishness. Within a few months she lost her job and began stealing to pay for the next hit. She spent all her money on drugs, which wrecked her body. She lost sixty pounds. Then Miriam became a dealer to make enough money to keep buying drugs. As her life spiraled out of control, Stephanie and Robert lived with their grand-mother on their mother's side, and Ray (Reginaldo) lived with his grandmother on his father's side because Miriam couldn't (or wouldn't) take care of them.

By the time Stephanie entered high school, her mother's life revolved around getting high and getting enough money to buy drugs to get high again. Stephanie lived in shame because of her mother. When she and her friends sometimes saw Miriam on the street, Stephanie's friends made fun of her mom. Feeling abandoned, Stephanie tried sex in an attempt to feel loved by someone—or anyone. One of her brothers also had a drug addiction. Stephanie desperately needed a loving, stable mother, but she didn't want Miriam to come home with her drug habit.

Eventually, Miriam was arrested and spent two years in prison. When she got out, she was raped at gunpoint. She became so depressed that she tried to end her life, but every attempt failed. She checked into rehab again and again, but nothing worked. Everything about Miriam looked utterly hopeless.

On a New Year's Eve, Miriam came to our church drunk and high on cocaine. While others celebrated the new year, some of our female pastors spent time with Miriam, praying that the new year would bring the promise of renewed hope. A few days later, one of these pastors, Alice, dropped by where Miriam was living. Miriam was distraught. She moaned, "I've tried everything."

"Have you tried Jesus?" Alice responded?

She was caught off guard by the question and answered, "No."

Alice smiled. "Then you haven't tried everything yet."

Alice invited Miriam to go to the farm where other addicts and prostitutes were finding a fresh start. There, she heard about the grace of God found in Jesus Christ, and she trusted in Him. Along with other women finding meaning and wholeness, Miriam studied the Bible, prayed, and learned she had something to live for. But she also realized she had deeply hurt her three children. She wanted to talk to them, apologize for all the damage she had caused, and ask for their forgiveness. She wanted a second chance to be their mother, but she knew they had no reason to trust her. She had made plenty of promises before, and she had broken all of them.

Miriam was right—Stephanie, Ray, and Robert were highly skeptical when their mother told them about the changes in her life, but when Miriam graduated from the New Life for Women program at the farm, the three of them came out. They too heard the message of Christ, and as they watched their mother over the next weeks and months, her new honesty convinced them that the change was real. Two of them were so attracted to their mother's new way of life that they trusted in Jesus, and soon Miriam's mother and three cousins also found Christ.

The Lord began to work deeply in Stephanie's life. She had looked for love in the arms of men, but she now had the courage to chart a new course for her life. She got involved in our church, and she found people who loved her without strings attached. When she graduated from high school, she entered our discipleship program called the Chicago Master's Commission.

On the seventh anniversary of the day Miriam ran into our church on New Year's Eve, Stephanie was anointed as a minister. Today she is serving God with joy, wisdom, and power. Her life is a testimony that no one—not her mother, not herself—is beyond the reach of God's great love. Miriam and Stephanie are shining lights in a dark world. Because they've been there, they have amazing empathy for people who are on the verge of giving up, and they have limitless hope for those people because they've seen God work miracles to change lives, especially their own.

It's easy to draw a line to exclude people because of their behavior or their views on important topics. It's important for us to develop a kingdom perspective about people and ideas. That's the only way to build bridges of love.

INSIDERS OR OUTSIDERS?

As she saw her mother throwing her life away and being so caught up in drugs that she wasn't even around, Stephanie was close to giving up on Miriam. It's completely understandable that she felt that way, but was it right?

Most of us have family members whose lives have gone off the rails. The list is almost endless: those who are alcoholics, addicts, thieves, liars, narcissists, hoarders, or sexual predators; human volcanoes who blow up and go dormant until the next explosion; people who are abusive; those who abandon us physically or emotionally; people who are irresponsible; and people with obsessive-compulsive habits or personality disorders, to name a few.

> It's important for us to develop a kingdom perspective about people and ideas. That's the only way to build bridges of love.

It's my guess that most of us have drawn a line in the sand, and on the other side are people we've written off as utterly hopeless. We barely put up with people who are habitually grouchy or whose habits are somewhat repulsive, but these others are beyond our limits.

To move the line so we can love more people, we need a rare and precious commodity: humility. In one of the most beautiful passages in the Bible, Paul describes the humility of Christ in his letter to the Philippians. Before this passage, though, he says that we can have a similar attitude if our hearts are filled with God's grace. Paul begins with a series of "if" statements, and the only appropriate answer is "Certainly!"

> Therefore if you have any encouragement from being united with Christ, if any comfort from his love, if any common sharing in the Spirit, if any tenderness and compassion...
>
> —PHILIPPIANS 2:1

Paul is reminding us of the phenomenal gift of grace poured out on us in Jesus. This grace isn't just a theological truth; it connects us with His heart so that contempt for others melts away and is replaced with kindness.

Notice that the "if" clauses conclude with a "then" statement as Paul describes what happens in us and through us when we experience grace:

> ...then make my joy complete by being like-minded, having the same love, being one in spirit and of one mind. Do nothing out of selfish ambition or vain conceit. Rather, in humility value others above yourselves, not looking to your own interests but each of you to the interests of the others. In your relationships with one another, have the same mindset as Christ Jesus.
>
> —PHILIPPIANS 2:2–5

What was Jesus' mindset? He didn't insist on His comfort and popularity. Instead, He emptied Himself. He was the King of glory, but He became a servant. He was the Lord of life, but He let Himself be killed to pay the penalty we deserved. He was supremely powerful, but He humbled himself for you and me. He died for His enemies, people who had nothing to offer, people like you and me.

We get a picture of how wide Jesus' love was on the morning of the resurrection. The first person who saw Christ was Mary Magdalene. When she saw Him, she didn't expect to see a risen Savior. She thought He was the gardener who had taken the body away. Jesus gently called her name, "Mary," and she knew it was Him. (See John 20:11–16.) At that moment, the message of the gospel was in the hands of a woman who, Luke tells us, had been possessed by seven demons (Luke 8:2). She was the most unlikely evangelist: she was a woman in a man's world, a person who had been possessed by demons, and uneducated. But Jesus looked beyond these factors and revealed Himself to her. You and I were just as unlikely, and He has revealed Himself to us.

Jesus obliterated the line and the limitations on His love. No one was outside His grace, and everyone was welcome to experience the wealth of His kindness. As we grasp His love more fully, our line will move out.

Does this mean we totally accept everyone, no matter how abusive or irresponsible he or she is? No, not exactly. We are called to love people but not necessarily to trust them. It would be foolish to trust an abuser or a habitual liar. Jesus loved the Pharisees by speaking the truth to them and letting them respond. Similarly, the way we love some people is to call them to account for their behavior and ask them to repent. That's the very best thing for them. They may not see it as loving, but it's the path of forgiveness and restoration—with God and with us. Love is limitless, but trust is based on proven responsibility; wisdom knows how to navigate these difficult relationships.

We can build bridges with people if they'll open their hearts—even just a little—so we can take steps toward each other. The relationship between Miriam and Stephanie looked utterly hopeless, but God made a way when neither of them saw one.

CULTURAL ISSUES

The divisions we have today are often about values, perspectives, and assumptions regarding the way life should work. People often ask me for my views on a wide variety of issues. Many people want clear, simple answers to complex problems, but this approach seldom leads to meaningful dialogue and compromises that bring real solutions. In fact, the polarization of politics today has made compromise a curse word, a sign of weakness, and something to be avoided at all costs. While taking that approach may sound strong and noble, it leads only to more resentment and stagnation.

> Love is limitless, but trust is based on proven responsibility; wisdom knows how to navigate these difficult relationships.

The trend toward tolerating others' choices and lifestyles is rooted in the belief that there is no ultimate truth—truth is relative: I have mine, you have yours, and they're equally valid. We don't want anyone to tell us we're wrong, and we don't want to offend others by telling them they're wrong. So, we accept every belief as equal.

That's not what Jesus, Paul, Peter, John, James, and the prophets taught! Again and again they attest not only to the truth of the Bible but also to its power. The writer to the Hebrews explains that God's Word has the ability to shine the light of truth into the crevasses of our souls.

> For the word of God is alive and active. Sharper than any double-edged sword, it penetrates even to dividing soul and spirit, joints and marrow; it judges the thoughts and attitudes of the heart. Nothing in all creation is hidden from God's sight. Everything is uncovered and laid bare before the eyes of him to whom we must give account.
>
> —Hebrews 4:12–13

Seminary president John Walvoord comments, "The Bible is God's declaratory revelation to man containing the great truths about God, about man, about history, about salvation, and about prophecy that God wanted us to know. The Bible could be trusted just as much as if God had taken the pen and written the words Himself."[1]

The Bible is our true north, the point that determines the direction of our lives. When Jesus was tempted by Satan, He quoted Scripture. When He was asked what's most important to God, He pointed to Scripture. His parables often paralleled passages found in the prophets. In the Sermon on the Mount, He contrasted "You have heard that it was said" with "But I tell you." On the cross He quoted a psalm in His anguish. No, for Jesus, all truth wasn't relative.

When people stand up for truth, they become lightning

rods. Today it seems that every post on social media invites backlash. Even those who eloquently advocate the values of God's kingdom are vilified by Christians (and unbelievers) who think they're not sufficiently outraged. Racial justice should be the easiest topic to draw us together, but we can catch heat even for referring to passages such as Ephesians 2, where Paul describes the unity of all races in the body of Christ. If Jesus is our example of grace, He's also our example of courage. He spoke God's truth and was killed. Centuries later another great leader, Abraham Lincoln, faced severe opposition from both political parties as he led the nation through the Civil War. Some blamed him for being radical; others vilified him for not moving fast enough. He changed the nature of the war by issuing a proclamation to free the slaves, and he was prepared to offer generous terms of reconciliation to the South. He was vilified by both sides during the war, but his public messages brought hope to a ravaged land...until he was murdered.

Dietrich Bonhoeffer was a Lutheran pastor in Germany as Hitler came to power and launched the war in Europe. He could have fled to America to find safety, but he returned to his homeland to stand up for Christ and resist the Nazis. He was arrested for his active opposition to Hitler, and he remained strong and joyful until he was executed shortly before the end of the war.

Martin Luther King Jr. was the lion of the civil rights movement. He endured taunts, threats, and attacks for saying that all men, including all people of color, are created equal. He was gunned down on the balcony of a hotel in Memphis.

Truth always wins. Standing up for what's true requires humility and courage—humility to refuse to hate and courage to keep speaking the truth in the face of opposition. It's easy to move to the extremes of blind hatred on one end or blind acceptance on the other. We need inner strength to wade into controversial topics with an open mind and a full heart, with the willingness to admit when we don't have good answers, the humility to confess when we're wrong, and the power to keep speaking the truth in the face of harsh and unfair treatment by some who disagree with us. If we speak the truth with humility, each conversation is another piece of the bridge between us and others.

WALK A MILE

It's a tried and true principle that if you want to understand people, you need to walk a mile in their shoes. That doesn't mean you need to adopt their positions, but it requires a large measure of empathy.

You don't just want to assume you're right and they're wrong and write them off. Instead, you want to do the hard work of understanding them, talking, listening, asking questions, and listening more. Here's a good measuring stick: unless you can articulate their positions as well as they can, you don't yet understand them well enough. In these rich discussions, you may not change their minds, but you may convince them that the God

> Jesus didn't have a list of people who were off-limits. No matter who they were, where they came from, or what they'd done, He built bridges and loved them anyway.

we love and serve isn't threatened by their positions. And you might just become friends with them in spite of your differences.

Jesus was called "a friend of tax collectors and sinners" (Luke 7:34). I have friends who are gay, friends who
are liberal Democrats, and friends who are conservative
Republicans. Some of my friends believe that climate change
is real; others think it's a hoax. Some believe Fox News is the
only source of truth, while others complain that the network
is the right's propaganda mouthpiece. These friends know I
agree with them on some issues and disagree on others, but
our differences don't drive us apart. In fact, they lead to wonderful conversations. But our discussions can be wonderful
only because we're respectful. Nobody has to win—or likely
will win—but we can still walk away and be friends.

No matter who we are, we can learn more about having
these sorts of rich conversations. For me, some of the most
important lessons are these:

- Give eye contact. This lets people know you're
  connecting.

- Ask open-ended questions that invite vulnerability and explanations, not yes or no answers.

- Focus on the person's last thought, not your
  next thought. Too often, we're thinking about
  the next thing we want to say when the other
  person is talking. Instead of sharing your convictions or changing the subject, ask follow-up
  questions.

- Discover the other person's interests. People
  love to talk about their particular skills and the
  issues they care about.

- Affirm without being phony. Look for appropriate times to say, "That's a good point," "You're really good at that," or "You understand that better than I do."

- Talk less and listen more. If your goal is understanding rather than being understood, you'll spend much more time listening.

If you practice these principles, you can have good conversations with almost anyone. I have a friend who is adamant that Puerto Rico should be liberated and become a sovereign nation. He's a liberal Democrat, so we disagree about a lot more than nationhood for our homeland. I love getting together with him for lunch from time to time. I know I'll be stimulated and challenged. We have animated discussions, and we may even get a little loud sometimes. But there's no hostility, no defensiveness, no sarcastic passive-aggressive behavior to punish the other person while we're smiling— none of that. When we end our lunches, we hug each other and look forward to our next time together.

Jesus didn't have a list of people who were off-limits. No matter who they were, where they came from, or what they'd done, He built bridges and loved them anyway. That's what I'm trying to do too.

DISCUSSION QUESTIONS

- For most people you know, where is the line between insiders and outsiders? Where is that line for you?

- Read Philippians 2:1–11. From Paul's if-then statements, what is the source of humility? From the passage, what effect does humility have on relationships? Where and how do you see this actually lived out? If you don't see it, explain what you think it would look like.

- Why is it important to distinguish between limitless love and limited trust? When you trust irresponsible people, what happens to you and what happens to them?

- Which of the hot topics I raised is an issue between you and someone you love? How does it affect your relationship?

- What does it mean to walk a mile in someone's shoes? How can you grow in empathy?

ACTION POINT: WHAT LOVE LOOKS LIKE

Take someone who disagrees with you about an important cultural issue to get a cup of coffee, and explain that you want to understand his or her point of view. When you get together, don't criticize and don't even share your opinion. Instead, ask this: "What's your hope for people who are affected by this issue? What do you think we can do to solve the problem? What do you wish I'd do about it?" And then listen.

CHAPTER 9

DRINK FROM THE RIGHT HOSE

As I spent time with people in our community, I saw the same attitudes among my neighbors as I saw on news broadcasts: to a great degree, anger had replaced love, suspicion had taken the place of trust, and mutual respect was a thing of the past.

I devoted a series in our church to the need to honor people around us instead of finding fault or ignoring them. On the last Sunday, we honored people who represented three groups that are often taken for granted. At our first service, we honored an eighth grader who had perfect attendance for two straight years. We brought him up on stage, talked about his remarkable accomplishment, and gave him a computer. Then we blessed him and prayed for him.

In the second service, we invited a young white guy who coaches an inner-city team at a local high school. The kids loved him like a father. It was a pleasure to tell our people how this young man had such a positive impact on the kids playing for him.

In the last service, I took a risk. I wanted to honor the unselfish service of someone who delivers pizza. I asked one of our staff members to order two large pizzas and have them delivered to our service at 12:30. We had no idea who would show up with the pizzas, of course, but at exactly 12:30, a black lady arrived at our church doors, holding an insulated brown bag containing two hot pizzas. A staff member welcomed her and escorted her to the stage where I was standing in front of the congregation. The church was packed. Every eye was on her, and she looked really nervous. I introduced myself: "I'm Pastor Choco. What's your name?"

She spoke softly, "Monique."

"Good to meet you, Monique. I'm the pastor of this church. I'm teaching a series on honoring people." I paused for a second and asked her, "What do you normally get as a tip when you deliver pizza?"

"Usually $5."

"Please hold out your hand." I peeled off ten 10-dollar bills and stacked them in her right palm. She was thrilled. That was supposed to be the end of the service, but instead, I turned to our congregation and said, "I'd like ten people to come up and honor Monique with a tip. Who will do that?"

People started walking up onto the stage and handing Monique money they had in their pockets and purses. I counted off the number of people and then said, "Thank you. That's ten."

But they kept coming. There must have been twenty, then thirty, and then forty members of our church congregation who came onto the stage and dropped dollar bills of different denominations into Monique's hand. By this time, Monique was weeping. While more people came up to present her money, I told her they were giving because they love Jesus and they loved her. She was overwhelmed with the kindness and generosity of people she didn't even know. Then I asked her to tell us what the gifts meant to her. Through her tears, she told us, "Thank you so much. I'm a single parent with two kids. I love my kids, and I'm trying to do my best."

We gave her a Bible and some other gifts, and before she went to her next delivery, I told her, "Monique, you are always welcome at this church. We want you to remember that you were marked by God on this day. It could have been any other pizza restaurant, and it could have been any other delivery person. But He chose you." We thanked God for her and prayed for her and her children. It was a glorious moment in her life and in the life of our church.

We video our services, and our social media team posted the video of our interactions with Monique. The next morning, someone called me and shouted, "The video has already gotten three hundred thousand views!"

"What are you talking about?" I asked.

"Monique, the pizza lady, on the stage," the social media team member replied. "It was posted last night, and three hundred thousand people have looked at it!" By the afternoon, a million had viewed the video. After a few weeks, a couple million people had seen the love poured out on Monique.[1] As of this writing, that number has passed 6.6 million views on Facebook.

All of us drink from a fountain that either nourishes or poisons us. In the series I taught at our church, I wanted our people to drink from a hose of gratitude, grace, and generosity. In our service that day, Monique drank from a hose of grace, and it touched her deeply.

159

We all drink from hoses at one time or another, and we hold the hose for other people as they drink. When we want to grow in our love for God and people, we need to step back and take a good look at what's coming out of the hose we're drinking from. After all, what we drink fills our hearts, and "out of the abundance of the heart [the] mouth speaks" (Luke 6:45, ESV). It's an inescapable truth: what we drink is what overflows into the lives of others.

FAUCETS OF POISON

I could identify an almost limitless variety of sources of information and values disguised as truth, but I'll focus on a few that I call faucets of poison. Here they are:

1. Social media

A 2018 survey reports that the average internet user spends three hours and forty-eight minutes a day online, with younger people online even more.[2] A number of factors attract people to various social media sites and apps and keep them there. One is the high a person gets from a like or, more specifically, enough likes. That's addictive! Positive responses trigger powerful chemicals in the brain that make people hungry for more. Psychologist Emma Kenny explains, "It's a reward cycle. You get a squirt of dopamine every time you get a like or a positive response on social media."[3]

Comparison is another factor that hooks people to social media and makes them dissatisfied with their own lives. Envy is a hot fire in the human heart, and social media pours gas on the flames.[4] People almost invariably post their most delicious and attractive meals, the most spectacular scenes from a vacation, and the biggest smiles on the faces of their family and friends. They don't post a first-thing-in-the-morning selfie, the peanut-butter-and-jelly-sandwich lunches inside a cubicle, waiting in long, boring traffic jams, or the arguments they have with people they love.

One of the most powerful attractions of social media, though, is being able to express anger, and angry posts have a good chance of going viral. Jonah Berger, a University of Pennsylvania marketing professor, concludes, "Anger is a high-arousal emotion, which drives people to take action....It makes you feel fired up, which makes you more likely to pass things on."[5]

In recent years, the level of anger online has skyrocketed. Researchers have shown that this anger is contagious. Fury and wrath trigger a burst of adrenaline that heightens your awareness of the danger posed by the people who oppose you, which makes you more likely to respond with a post that's at least as angry as the one you just read. Dr. Gary Slutkin, a University of Illinois at Chicago faculty member and founder of Cure Violence, says that "violence and violent speech meet the criteria of disease. Like a virus, violence makes more of itself. Rage begets more rage. And it spreads because we humans are wired to follow our peers."[6]

Social media has given a platform to everyone, from the one who has thirty followers to the one who has thirty million. Everyone has an opportunity to spew anger or communicate love. Sadly, anger wins far too often. People become intoxicated with the envy and anger that is so prevalent on the most-frequented sites, and they can't stop perpetuating it.

2. The news media

Nearly everyone watches and listens to news outlets that confirm what he or she already believes, and the same factors that propel individuals' immersion in social media are at work as they soak up the commentary on these programs. Let's face it: because we love drama and most of us don't want to be bored by detailed analysis of complicated topics, we gravitate to the broadcasts and broadcasters who confirm our worldview—and inflame our emotions. A few programs make a concerted effort to present both sides and provide in-depth analysis. These are the ones we need to pay more attention to.[7]

3. The enemy

Many of us have difficulty discerning the attacks from Satan, the enemy of our souls, from the ingrained negative input from our past. Actually we don't need to draw any lines between them because Satan often uses those painful messages to distract us, confuse us, and crush us.

Keep in mind that Satan has three primary avenues of attack: deception, temptation, and accusation. The problem is that he usually uses our own internal voice to communicate these destructive messages.

Jesus said Satan is "a liar and the father of lies" (John 8:44). It's his nature to deceive people, first to keep them from grasping the truth of the gospel and then to keep Christians from living in that truth. He puts thoughts in our minds that God can't possibly love us because of the sins we've committed, that we're helpless and hopeless, and that we're doomed to a dead-end life. These thoughts often are in the form of "I" statements. Here are a few examples:

- "I'm such a loser."

- "I can't afford to be wrong or I'll look like a fool."

- "I'm all alone. No one cares about me."

- "No matter how hard I try, it's never enough."
- "If that certain person isn't pleased with me, I just can't live with myself."
- "I'm worthless, unloved, and unlovable."

When these lies take root in our hearts, we are easily tempted to pursue meaning and happiness from other sources. We try to fill the gaping hole in our hearts with power, pleasure, or popularity, but no matter how beautiful or handsome we look, how much money we have, or how much acclaim we receive, the satisfaction never lasts. We always become empty again and long for more. The cycle never stops until something far better fills our hearts.

Accusations are often internalized messages we've heard from others, and we conclude they're true:

- "I'm such a fool."
- "I'll never make it."
- "I'm ugly."
- "I'm stupid."
- "I can't do anything right."

Some of us live with these tapes playing over and over in our minds, even as we go to church, sing songs of praise, and read the Bible. Somehow, these messages seem more powerful and more valid than the truth of Scripture.

But they aren't, and that's because the Lord is our stronghold.

SWEET WATER

When Elisha succeeded Elijah as God's prophet in Israel, his first act was to address a problem of bitter water that didn't allow farmers to cultivate their fields.

> The people of the city said to Elisha, "Look, our lord, this town is well situated, as you can see, but the water is bad and the land is unproductive."
>
> "Bring me a new bowl," he said, "and put salt in it." So they brought it to him.
>
> Then he went out to the spring and threw the salt into it, saying, "This is what the LORD says: 'I have healed this water. Never again will it cause death or make the land unproductive.'" And the water has remained pure to this day, according to the word Elisha had spoken.
>
> —2 KINGS 2:19–22

The new bowl symbolized that God was going to do something new, and salt was a preservative and cleansing agent.

This is exactly what we need God to do for us today: to change the bitter waters of hateful, sarcastic, contemptuous messages to sweet waters of love, kindness, and justice. We need to drink from these sweet waters, and we need to hold the hose so others can drink from them as well. Of course, this means we have to be observant and strong to filter out the bitter and let in only the sweet. Does the church have the power to turn bitter water into sweet? Do we even notice that we're drinking bitter water and giving it to others?

The source of sweet water is obvious: God and His Word. Far too often, we sip from the Bible and stand in front of the fire hose of social media, divisive news outlets, and Satan's attacks. We need to stand in front of different hoses!

As we've seen, Jesus offers a different fountain than the one most of us drink from. He began by acknowledging the common understanding of believers in His day.

> You have heard that it was said, "Love your neighbor and hate your enemy." But I tell you, love your enemies and pray for those who persecute you.
>
> —MATTHEW 5:43–44

The Bible has a lot to say about how we should treat the people we love. We don't just say we love them; we're to bless them.

Doing so is far more than words. This means taking action to meet their needs, affirm them, and validate their worth—even if we disagree with them. We can speak the truth about their irresponsible behavior, but we don't have the right to blast them simply for holding views different from ours. Paul told the Christians in Thessalonica, "And we urge you, brothers and sisters, warn those who are idle and disruptive, encourage the disheartened, help the weak, be patient with everyone" (1 Thess. 5:14).

Instead of all the anger and fear we see in families and among Christians, we need to remember the standard God gave His people for relationships. The prophet Micah told the people:

> He has shown you, O mortal, what is good. And what does the LORD require of you? To act justly and to love mercy and to walk humbly with your God.
>
> —MICAH 6:8

Is that how people who disagree with us see us? If not, we're failing to follow God's path and express His heart.

Today, the inflammatory rhetoric is poisoning our relationships. There is a generational divide, and a lot of our kids hold beliefs and values different from ours. We can try to badger them into agreeing with us, or we can try to understand their positions. And this may surprise you, but sometimes, their views are more in line with the Bible than ours.

We could look at a number of issues to see what the sweet water of God's truth says about them, but I want to focus on the disadvantaged. Many conservatives are outraged at what they view as "government handouts" and overly generous assistance programs. Yet the Bible says that God has a special place in His heart for those who are on the margins.

God spoke through the prophet Zechariah to identify four specific vulnerable populations: the widow, the fatherless, the foreigner, and the poor. He wanted His people to show these individuals justice, mercy, and compassion" (Zech. 7:9–10).

In a similar but much longer passage, God spoke through Isaiah to correct His people's idea of what He wanted from them. They complained that they had done everything God had asked them to do, and they accused Him of not noticing how humble they were. (That's never a good angle when we communicate with God!) They insisted they had gone to great lengths to prove their loyalty to God by fasting, but God tells them they completely missed His heart.

> Is not this the kind of fasting I have chosen: to loose
> the chains of injustice and untie the cords of the yoke,
> to set the oppressed free and break every yoke? Is it not
> to share your food with the hungry and to provide the

poor wanderer with shelter—when you see the naked, to clothe them, and not to turn away from your own flesh and blood?

—Isaiah 58:6–7

God was telling them to notice the plight of the disadvantaged and take action to meet their needs. God says that these people are "your own flesh and blood." We may have different skin colors, different backgrounds, and different faiths, but all of us are created in God's image—we're all part of the family of human beings. We should treat everyone like beloved members of our own families because, in God's sight, that's who they are.

Do angry Christians today demonstrate the life of Christ? It's good to be righteously indignant, but godly anger primarily should be directed at injustice that harms others. Far too often, we're furious that we're the victims of injustice, and we don't seem to care that others suffer. But if we allow God to change our hearts with His love for us so that we have plenty of love to share with the disadvantaged, we'll experience the wonder of His presence, as God's Word reminds us.

If you do away with the yoke of oppression, with the pointing finger and malicious talk, and if you spend yourselves in behalf of the hungry and satisfy the needs of the oppressed, then your light will rise in the darkness, and your night will become like the noonday. The Lord will guide you always; he will satisfy your needs in a sun-scorched land and will strengthen your frame. You will be like a well-watered garden, like a spring whose waters never fail.

—Isaiah 58:9–11

We certainly need good governmental policies, but Christians need to insist that these policies be shaped by the values of humility and generosity. It's my responsibility and privilege to follow Jesus and care for people He loves. Matthew gives us another glimpse into His heart.

> Jesus went through all the towns and villages, teaching in their synagogues, proclaiming the good news of the kingdom and healing every disease and sickness. When he saw the crowds, he had compassion on them, because they were harassed and helpless, like sheep without a shepherd. Then he said to his disciples, "The harvest is plentiful but the workers are few. Ask the Lord of the harvest, therefore, to send out workers into his harvest field."
>
> —MATTHEW 9:35–38

Jesus told His disciples to ask the Lord of the harvest to send out people to care for His sheep. Are you an answer to this prayer?

FILTERING MESSAGES

We can't completely escape the poisonous messages in our culture, but we can be far more active in filtering them. At our house, I have to change the air filter regularly, or it becomes clogged and ineffective. We need to do a lot better at filtering out the bitter and filtering in the sweet. It's a simple concept, but it requires courage and tenacity.

We have developed habits that seem unchangeable. We read the same journalists, listen to the same commentators, and watch the same news. And our friends (the ones we're most comfortable with because they agree with us) read, listen to, and watch the same opinion makers. Change may be hard, but it's necessary. In some cases, the change is simply to avoid letting those messages in. Turn off the radio, change the channel, or read something else. Or the change may be to find sources that are more in line with God's heart and values.

I want to ask a pointed question: Are your values and passions shaped more by the media than by the Word of God? Do your words and your actions reflect God's compassion for the disadvantaged, or are they mirrors of the voices coming from the political right or left?

I've pointed out some Old Testament passages about the priority of caring for those who need help, and I find the same priority in the New Testament. Not long before His arrest and crucifixion, Jesus told a parable about those who are considered righteous and those who aren't. Referring to Himself as the King, Jesus said that He would separate His people into two groups. To those on His right, the King says:

> Come, you who are blessed by my Father; take your inheritance, the kingdom prepared for you since the creation of the world. For I was hungry and you gave me something to eat, I was thirsty and you gave me something to drink, I was a stranger and you invited me in, I needed clothes and you clothed me, I was sick and you looked after me, I was in prison and you came to visit me.
>
> —MATTHEW 25:34–36

Those people are surprised by the King's statement. They can't imagine when they had cared for Him. They ask, "Lord, when did we see you hungry and feed you, or thirsty and give you something to drink? When did we see you a stranger

169

and invite you in, or needing clothes and clothe you? When did we see you sick or in prison and go to visit you?" (Matt. 25:37–39).

The King answers, "Truly I tell you, whatever you did for one of the least of these brothers and sisters of mine, you did for me" (v. 40).

But the King isn't finished with his pronouncements. He turns to the people on his left and says, "Depart from me, you who are cursed, into the eternal fire prepared for the devil and his angels. For I was hungry and you gave me nothing to eat, I was thirsty and you gave me nothing to drink, I was a stranger and you did not invite me in, I needed clothes and you did not clothe me, I was sick and in prison and you did not look after me" (vv. 41–43).

They protest that they had never seen the King in need, but He tells them, "Truly I tell you, whatever you did not do for one of the least of these, you did not do for me" (v. 45).

Jesus explained the result of having and not having compassion for those in need: "Then they will go away to eternal punishment, but the righteous to eternal life" (v. 46).

Jesus couldn't be clearer—or more challenging. If our words and actions don't reflect the compassion and active care of Jesus, there's reason to wonder if we know Him at all.

HOW TO CHANGE

Throughout the Bible, we see people who were going in the wrong direction, realized it, and made a change. The prodigal son "came to his senses" in the pigpen and started walking toward home (Luke 15:17); he made a change. Another word for change is *repentance*. It means to change our agenda. We see that we're valuing the wrong things or our behavior dishonors God, and we make the necessary adjustments. We admit our error, thank God for His forgiveness, and chart a new path. A familiar passage in Jeremiah illustrates the heart of repentance.

> This is what the LORD says: "Let not the wise boast of their wisdom or the strong boast of their strength or the rich boast of their riches, but let the one who boasts boast about this: that they have the understanding to know me, that I am the LORD, who exercises kindness, justice and righteousness on earth, for in these I delight," declares the LORD.
>
> —JEREMIAH 9:23–24

What do people see us boast in? Do we boast that God, in His infinite grace, has chosen us to be His beloved children? And do we point people to His qualities of kindness, justice, and righteousness? Our boast is like a hose. We hold it in front of others for them to drink, and it carries either bitter water or sweet.

Jesus couldn't be clearer—or more challenging. If our words and actions don't reflect the compassion and active care of Jesus, there's reason to wonder if we know Him at all.

When we drink from the wrong hose, our thirst isn't quenched, and if we drink from it long enough, we get into big trouble. In Psalm 42, the writer compares spiritual thirst with a deer dying from lack of water.

> As the deer pants for streams of water, so my soul pants for you, my God. My soul thirsts for God, for the living God. When can I go and meet with God?
>
> —PSALM 42:1–2

Water is life. Our bodies can't manufacture it; it has to come from outside, and we can't live more than a couple of days without it. When people are dehydrated, their vision may blur, they feel lightheaded and fatigued, and their mouths become dry; severe dehydration causes organ failure and can be deadly.[8] The psalmist gives us a picture of a deer near death because it can't find water, which is a parallel of what happens to us when we don't drink deeply from the living water of Jesus.

RESTORED RELATIONSHIPS

Drinking from the wrong source invariably creates relational problems. Our resentment and self-pity have driven people away, confused them, and hurt them. We may have tried to dominate them, given in to their intimidation, or avoided them, but any of these behaviors drive a wedge between us and them. Or much of the problem may lie on the other side, and we feel abandoned or brutalized. (And it's almost always a two-way street.)

Either way, the fabric of the relationship is torn, but it doesn't have to stay that way. God has given us the balm of His grace to forgive us, and He has given us a process to mend the rifts, restore love, and rebuild trust with others.

We can come up with a dozen excuses to delay, but Jesus encourages us to act with a sense of urgency: "Therefore, if you are offering your gift at the altar and there remember that your brother or sister has something against you, leave your gift there in front of the altar. First go and be reconciled to them; then come and offer your gift" (Matt. 5:23–24). Jesus also said, "If your brother or sister sins, go and point out their fault, just between the two of you. If they listen to you, you have won them over" (18:15).

In other words, whether you are the offender or the one offended, it's up to you to take the first step to make things right. We are fallen people who live in a fallen world, so it's safe to assume that all of us have offended people at many instances in our distant and recent past. We don't want to admit it because we don't like to be wrong or we don't want the awkwardness of these conversations, but repentance is the lifeblood of the Christian life. We need to become proficient at it if we want our lives to represent the One who died so that we could be reconciled to God.

When we bring our "gift" to the altar, we're bringing much more than our money. We're bringing our hearts, our lives, our desires, and our choices. Paul told the Roman Christians to offer their bodies (which represented everything about them) to God: "Therefore, I urge you, brothers and sisters, in view of God's mercy, to offer your bodies as a living sacrifice, holy and pleasing to God—this is your true and proper worship" (Rom. 12:1).

We worship God and honor Him by giving everything we are, everything we do, and everything we have to Him. This moment-by-moment choice requires radical reconstruction of our thinking, which requires us to drink from the right hose. Paul instructed us, "Do not conform to the pattern of this world, but be transformed by the renewing of your mind. Then you will be able to test and approve what God's will is—his good, pleasing and perfect will" (v. 2).

In families, trust may have been eroded by constant criticism or emotional neglect, or it could have been shattered by physical, emotional, or sexual abuse. Forgiveness is one-way, but reconciliation requires both people to take steps forward. It's our responsibility to offer the path and see if the person is willing to go with us.

In the church, we find people who are annoying and those who have made themselves our enemies. We need to put up with the one and boldly address the other. We should take the initiative to forgive, and we should seek understanding, meaningful connections, and peace between us and the other individuals. Months and years of sarcasm, gossip, and suspicion have poisoned the water, but forgiveness and love can make the water sweet.

Sometimes, we're clueless that another person has been offended. A man came up to me a few years ago to tell me that I had hurt his feelings when we played basketball—and we were both fourteen at the time! I had no idea that he had harbored hurt for so long. But when he told me, I apologized and asked for forgiveness, and we parted without any hard feelings between us.

Reconciliation is a powerful statement to the community. In the winter of 2016, the weather forecast was for a week of brutal cold in the Windy City. People who live on the streets were going to suffer, and they already were facing what seemed to be indiscriminate violence. In addition, we saw a shocking increase in drug abuse, prostitution, and sex trafficking during this time.

We decided to address the problem with a three-week program we called Safety in the Sanctuary. We already had a ministry to go to the people who live on the streets and under bridges to provide resources for them and tell them about Jesus. In our new program, we opened our church doors so they could get out of the cold. We gave them a place to sleep, fed them, prayed with them, and joined them for games at night. Although our church hadn't ignored them or harmed them, they felt abandoned by society, and we wanted to make it right.

Of course, we had security around the clock to be sure people were safe. We enlisted teachers from the school near our church to serve meals, and local restaurants provided food. Our people eagerly got involved by bringing meals and staying to love on the ones who came. Volunteers came to help twenty-four hours a day, seven days a week, for the three weeks.

We understood we were taking a measure of risk letting street people into our building. Some of them came in high, and at least one shot up in our restroom. A large percentage of people who live on the street suffer from mental illness, and we provided referrals to nearby clinics to get them professional help.

For those who were strung out on drugs, we got them into a detox unit at a nearby hospital, and we coordinated medical care for those who were sick. Counseling agencies and shelters provided services and invited people to

> Love isn't love until it's demonstrated.

use their facilities. It took a lot of energy and time to care for people who came to us, but it was worth it all. A number of people came to Christ, and we baptized them. Family members came to the church to see their loved ones, and several families saw incredible reconciliation. One young woman heard about our ongoing program of discipleship, and she left the streets to participate in the Teen Center.

Later that year, we wanted to draw attention to the people

in Chicago who had lost their lives in violent crimes. We started a Love Life campaign. We asked people in our church to make white crosses, and with each police report of a homicide, we planted one on a hill next to our church campus. On each cross, we wrote the name and age of a person who had died. By that time, several hundred had been killed, and the hill began to fill with white crosses.

By the end of the year, 747 crosses crowded the hillside. We held a memorial and prayer vigil, and we invited the families of those who died to come, pray, sing, and cry. We often saw people walking through the rows of crosses to find the name of the person they'd lost, just like people walk through the cemeteries at Arlington or Normandy. Local news reported on our growing forest of crosses. Love Life honored the people who died and their families.

> If we wait until we feel like forgiving and reconciling before we make a move, we'll miss out on one of the greatest miracles God has for us: restored relationships.

In both of these efforts, we wanted to turn the hose of God's love toward our community to let them know we see them, we love them, and we reach out to them in ways that matter to them. Love isn't love until it's demonstrated. Jesus demonstrated His love for us. We had nothing to give, but while we were still sinners, Christ died for us (Rom. 5:8).

People often hear me say, "God says it. Just do it!" If we wait until we completely understand ourselves or our situations, we'll wait too long. If we wait until we have pleasant emotions before we take bold steps to change hoses, we'll keep drinking bitter water. If we wait until we feel like forgiving and reconciling before we make a move, we'll miss out on one of the greatest miracles God has for us: restored relationships. God's powerful work in our lives is attached to a set of instructions we find in the Bible. If we trust Him and follow these instructions, we tap into the power and love that caused the universe to spin into existence—an unstoppable power, an unquenchable love.

Obedience can't wait. Love them anyway. Love them now.

DISCUSSION QUESTIONS

- Describe how comparison and anger on social media are both addicting and destructive.

- If the enemy's messages to us are so negative, why do we believe them so easily?

- Read Isaiah 58:6–11. We looked at several passages in which God tells us to have compassion for the poor, for immigrants, and for other disadvantaged people. What would happen if Christians were convinced this is the kind of love that's essential in the kingdom of God? What would happen if you really believed it?

- What difference would it make if you experienced reconciliation with people you've offended or who have offended you? What would your next step be?

ACTION POINTS: WHAT LOVE LOOKS LIKE

Fast from social media for a week and see how doing that affects your outlook. Analyze your sources of input, and determine what hoses you're drinking from. Analyze the hoses your family members and friends are drinking from. Brainstorm with your friends or your small group to turn the hose of God's love on your community. Finally, take the first step of reconciliation by making the call or getting involved in a ministry.

CHAPTER 10

LOVE DEFEATS HATE

On January 11, 1989, tragedy struck our family. Elizabeth's father, Ignacio Marrero, was the pastor of our church, and she had five siblings. By that time, we had been married for over a year. Her younger brother, Ignacio (lovingly known as Nachito), had been at Elizabeth's parents' house talking with her dad. Her father asked him to help him clean the garage, but he said, "I'll help you on Saturday. I've made plans to see my friends today."

A couple of hours later, after returning home from worship rehearsal, Elizabeth received the earth-shattering news that Nachito had been shot and killed. We quickly drove to her father's house, and her father told her that it wasn't an accident: Nachito had been murdered when a fourteen-year-old boy shot him in a gang initiation. It seems that Nachito had been standing next to a really big guy who was a member of a local gang. The boy shot the other guy several times, but he lived. A single shot hit my brother-in-law Nachito, and this time the bullet wound was fatal.

The family was devastated. Elizabeth's parents were well

179

aware of the gangs in the neighborhood, so they were very protective. They didn't expect anything like this to happen to one of their children.

The boy had worn a ski mask when he shot Nachito, so no one could identify him. But he felt so guilty that he confessed to the crime a few days later. There was no trial, but on the day the judge sentenced him, Elizabeth and her sisters attended court. She looked across the courtroom at the boy's family, and she saw his mother weeping. Elizabeth instantly realized that two families were losing a son, one to death and the other to prison, and she had a heart full of compassion for his mother. Both families loved their sons and brothers, and they both grieved the senseless loss.

In a remarkable act of courage, Elizabeth's father chose to forgive the boy soon after the murder. He never spoke an unkind or bitter word about him. He wasn't stoic; he suffered deep grief, but in the middle of his pain, he forgave. Years later, when the family visited Ignacio's grave in Puerto Rico, Elizabeth's father wept at the gravesite. The loss didn't fade away, but neither did his sense of God's love, presence, and power.

Hating is easy; loving is hard. Ignacio had the strength of character to overwhelm any desire for revenge with enormous compassion for a boy who had made a tragic and foolish decision—a decision that cost the family their beloved son. But Ignacio still trusted God to fill the gaping hole in his heart.

Over the years, I've seen many Christian leaders quit when they suffered setbacks and losses. For them, the cost overcame the benefits of remaining in their roles, so they walked away. Elizabeth's father did the calculation, and he decided to stay—not as a bitter man who survived on the adrenaline of resentment but as a loving man who refused to let a young boy's rash and stupid decision wreck more than one life.

I watched Elizabeth's father continue to serve the church and the community through the deepest pain a father can experience. Like King David, who suffered the loss of his infant son and then picked himself up and returned to serve in his responsibilities, her dad

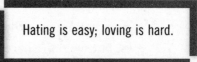

Hating is easy; loving is hard.

got up from the blow and kept caring, kept loving, and kept serving. His tenacity taught me that when people do things to destroy your hopes and shatter your joy, love them anyway. Don't let anger and bitterness crowd love out.

I heard my father-in-law preach often about the love of Jesus and the command to love our neighbors, and I saw him love the community—the community that produced the young man who killed his son. He had made a steadfast commitment to experience and express love no matter what life threw at him. To say the least, I was very impressed with his commitment.

A LIFESTYLE

In the church and business worlds, people go to conferences and read books to discover strategies for growth. That's why I say that love isn't a strategy; it's a lifestyle. You can't uncover "five surefire steps to love people" just like that. Jesus didn't give us a checklist to follow. He gave us Himself. We fail to love when we see people as "the other," but Jesus became "the other," identifying with those who are infinitely below

Him and loving us still. Moving forward, keep these points in mind:

- We may not approve of the lifestyle of gay or lesbian individuals, but they are not "the other." They're created in the image of God, and God loves them as much as He loves you and me.

- We may not agree with a person's political views, but we don't have to assume it's a character flaw to advocate for his or her positions. We don't know everything, and in fact we've been wrong far too often, which should bring us at least a hint of humility.

- We may be upset with the attitudes and behaviors of family members, but they need the grace and love of Jesus as much as we do.

Love breaks down the walls separating us from "the other." These people are more valuable to God than the stars in the sky. If we begin to see them the way God sees them, we'll start to love them the way He loves them. Many of us will need to admit that we have gone years professing Christ but have failed to love people. Let me tell you a few stories of people learning to love.

> When people do things to destroy your hopes and shatter your joy, love them anyway. Don't let anger and bitterness crowd love out.

A lady who joined our church came to my office one day weeping. She told me, "Pastor Choco, I've wasted so much of my life! I didn't love, and I didn't know how to love. I'm finally realizing how much God loves me and how I can love others."

She had been a member of another church for thirty-seven years, but during all that time, the church hadn't done much to care for people outside their walls. When she came to our church, she immediately got involved in feeding the poor and providing for the homeless.

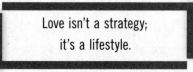

Love isn't a strategy; it's a lifestyle.

Her active service ignited her spiritual life. She experienced more love than she'd ever known before, and it poured out of her to people in need.

Matthew is a young man who was raised in a safe, white, affluent suburb of Chicago. His neighborhood was the polar opposite of Humboldt Park. When he enrolled in our church's Master's Commission, he instantly became a minority since he was the only white person in the program.

"Before I came, I never considered myself to be prejudiced," he told me, "but I was seldom around people who were very different from me. When I got here, I soon realized I had an unseen but very real sense of racial and cultural superiority. I had to face the fact that I really thought I was better than people with black or brown skin. I used sarcasm to distance myself from the people around me and subtly put them down. I always did it with a smile, but they knew—and I knew—that I thought I was better than them."

After a second or two, he continued, "The sarcasm was a cover for my insecurity. I didn't feel comfortable out of my culture, and this was the only way I knew to cope."

Matthew ruffled a lot of feathers in his first several months at the Master's Commission, but he didn't realize how he had offended people until another student confronted him. "At that moment," he explains, "I stood face to face with the ugliest part of me. I had belittled people so I could feel superior." He made a conscious choice to repent: to change his agenda, change his perspective, change his words, and change his relationships. He apologized to the people he had offended—which was just about everybody—and he made a concerted effort to speak words of affirmation instead of sarcastic condemnation.

"I still caught myself being sarcastic, but I was able to stop and apologize right away. People were very kind to encourage me as I trusted God to change me," Matthew said. He took a deep breath and added this final thought: "The transformation has been slower than I'd like, but it's happening. I'm grateful for that."

> Many of us will need to admit that we have gone years professing Christ but have failed to love people.

Anders, my son-in-law, is another young man who has learned a lot about love. A few years ago he had a roommate who was a big, strong guy who'd developed his physique by cutting down and hauling trees for his father's company. When the two roommates joked around, the big man liked to throw Anders around. One night he got a little too rough. When Anders tried to stop him, the bigger dude got really angry and threatening—which, to 140-pound Anders, was terrifying. They wrestled for a while, and then Anders pulled away and yelled, "You've got to get your anger under control! One day you're going to kill somebody! You'll spend the rest of your life in prison!"

Anders remembers that moment well. "At the time, I'd

been reading a book titled *Loving the Way Jesus Loves*," by Philip Ryken, he said. "It uses all the characteristics in 1 Corinthians 13 as a measuring stick to show us how much we love people. I instantly realized that my words to my roommate weren't even close. In the church, a lot of us believe the command to avoid hating is ironclad but the command to love is optional, so we settle for not hating.

"In reality if we refuse to love, we're actually hating. One of the points I really want to make is that 'love isn't irritable.' It was abundantly clear that I'd been irritable, and it didn't make any difference that my roommate had been irritable first. I was good at loving people who are easy to love and who love me, or at least like me, but I wasn't good at loving people who got on my nerves. I had become an expert at finding things about people that made them less than acceptable, so I excused myself for not loving them. But loving them isn't optional."

One of the most common perspectives is that the other side is full of bigots while our side is noble, godly, and pure. That's seldom, if ever, the case. The killing of George Floyd followed the deaths of dozens of other black men and women. What began as peaceful protests gave people opportunity to vent their outrage, and like Newton's law it produced an equal and opposite reaction. Both sides were absolutely sure they were right.

Because of slavery in this country, we often think of racism as a problem in the white community, but blacks, browns, Asians, Native Americans, and people of every other ethnicity can be just as prejudiced. A different error is that we often see the victims, but not the perpetrators, as worthy of love.

Sadly, our nation's football championship game has become a magnet for sex trafficking, and our church sends people to the city where it's played each year to help the girls get out of that kind of slavery. It's easy to love the women who are misused and abused, but it's also important to love the men who abuse them. Is our grasp of the love of God strong enough and wide enough to believe that pimps and johns are created in the image of God and are more valuable to Him than all the diamonds and gold found in the earth? If not, we haven't yet understood the depth of Jesus' amazing love for us.

Anders was one of the people from our church who traveled to the site of the football championship game. About two o'clock one morning, he drove a van of people to a strip club. The girls from the church went in to talk with the girls, and Anders stood in the parking lot waiting for them. A car drove up, and a young man got out. He walked up to Anders and asked, "Hey, what's the cover charge at this place?"

Anders told him, "I don't know. We're from a church in Chicago, and we're here to bless the women and let them know that Jesus loves them."

The guy looked stunned. He got back in his car and sat for a long time. Finally, he got out and approached Anders again. This time, he said, "You know, this was going to be the first time I've ever been to a strip club. I've struggled for years with pornography. I was hanging out with friends, and I decided tonight I was going to do it."

He stood for a few seconds with his head hung low, and then he looked at Anders and said, "I, uh, I used to be a youth pastor. I just couldn't overcome my addiction to porn, so I left the ministry. Tonight, seeing you here reminds me that there are people who are helping people find God. I came here to take my lust to the next level, but instead, would you pray for me?"

Anders later explained, "When I parked the van outside the strip club that night and looked at all the other cars, I assumed every man was selfish, abusive, and dirty. The guy who asked me to pray for him shows me that I don't know what's in the hearts of these people, and I can't know how God is already at work to draw them to Himself. If I make negative assumptions, I miss out on opportunities to point people to Jesus."

Jen is the product of a broken home, which left a gaping hole in her heart. She desperately wanted to love and be loved, but she made some very bad choices in relationships. Boyfriends verbally and physically abused her, crushing her spirit. One of them hit her behind closed doors and out in public. Of course, he apologized and promised to change (promises make victims believe things are going to be different, but they almost never are), but the physical abuse got only worse. She started doing drugs to numb the pain and fit in, and she got hooked on heroin. Before long, she was arrested and served time in prison. In her misery, she shut herself off from every relationship. She didn't trust anyone.

God used Jen's sister's father-in-law to become a surrogate dad, stepping into her life with kindness and consistency. Gradually, she realized this was a man who wasn't going to hurt her and didn't want anything from her. Jen found Christ and a new source of stability. The love she experienced from her surrogate dad was, she realized, an example of the endless love God has for her. The emotional wounds began to heal, and she gained wisdom about whom to trust and how to love.

Years ago, Promise Keepers held a conference at Soldier Field in Chicago for almost 70,000 men. A man in the audience listened carefully as one of the speakers talked passionately about racial reconciliation. He didn't think the message related to him because he was sure he wasn't prejudiced toward anyone. He was a Puerto Rican, but he had friends who were all colors and from different national origins. The speaker asked the audience to get up and make a physical demonstration of their unity by hugging people who looked different from them. All over the stadium, men from different ethnic and racial backgrounds hugged each other. During this time, the Holy Spirit whispered to the man in the audience, "Sure, you get along with people who aren't like you, but you don't really love them."

Instantly, he knew what the Spirit was saying was true. His mind went back to instances in his past of running away from white kids who wanted to beat him up and being scared of gangs of blacks. He had avoided them for years, and he had learned to tolerate them. But the Spirit was asking a different question. It wasn't "Do you despise them?" He could say no to that. But this was "Do you love them?" and he realized he didn't. He went to the altar to pray and confess his sin of not loving his neighbor, and then he got up and hugged every man within reach.

That man was me. God was moving in my heart to prepare me to be a minister of reconciliation in Humboldt Park and beyond, but first, he had to work a miracle of repentance in my heart. A lifestyle of loving people across racial barriers began that day.

THE SURPRISE OF LOVE

Not long after Jesus rose from the tomb and ascended back to the Father, the disciples were busy telling everyone who would listen about Jesus and helping the new believers grow in their faith.

One day as Peter and John were on their way to the temple to pray, they passed by a lame man who was being carried to the temple gate to beg. When he saw the two men, the lame man asked them for money. Peter told him, "Look at us!"

The beggar expected Peter to hand him a coin, but the apostle had a different offer: "Silver or gold I do not have, but what I do have I give you. In the name of Jesus Christ of Nazareth, walk" (Acts 3:6).

Peter took the man by the hand. Immediately, his feet and hands were strengthened, and he jumped to his feet. Luke, the author of Acts, tells us:

> Then he went with them into the temple courts, walking and jumping, and praising God. When all the people saw him walking and praising God, they recognized him as the same man who used to sit begging at the temple gate called Beautiful, and they were filled with wonder and amazement at what had happened to him.
>
> —Acts 3:8–10

Love propelled Peter to notice a man who had a chronic need and had given up on ever getting well. At that moment, Peter may have remembered that Jesus had reached out His hand to him when he stepped out of the boat to walk toward Him and began to sink (Matt. 14:31).

At the temple gate, the lame man received something he

never expected. It was a shock to him and to everyone else there. We don't know how much money Peter and John had on them. They may have had a contribution to give at the temple that day, or their pockets may have been empty. But they gave something we can always give—love.

Our church is known for outreach events in the community and mission trips to the far corners of the globe, but we know that something transformational happens when people work and serve together; love connects them. Our events are designed to give a lot of people the opportunity to love and be loved.

EVEN THERE, EVEN THEN, EVEN NOW

Too often today, the images of the church are of angry faces. Anger is rising up when love needs to rise up. Loving the people who threaten us or disagree with us is hard, but never forget that Jesus found a way.

In the middle of His ministry, Jesus took His disciples to Caesarea Philippi, a pagan region in the northern part of the country, far from the temple in Jerusalem. They were in enemy territory. Jesus asked them,

"Who do people say the Son of Man is?"

They replied, "Some say John the Baptist; others say Elijah; and still others, Jeremiah or one of the prophets."

"But what about you?" he asked. "Who do you say I am?"

Simon Peter answered, "You are the Messiah, the Son of the living God."

Jesus replied, "Blessed are you, Simon son of Jonah, for this was not revealed to you by flesh and blood, but by my Father in heaven. And I tell you that you are

Peter, and on this rock I will build my church, and the gates of Hades will not overcome it."

—MATTHEW 16:13–18

Jesus was saying that even where we're most threatened, He's the Messiah, the Son of the Living God. The place He took the disciples was named for Caesar, the Roman emperor, the most powerful ruler on earth, but Jesus was and is far more powerful. He spoke and the stars were flung into space. Nothing matches His supreme authority and power. The pagans believed Caesarea Philippi contained an entrance to the underworld, a dangerous place, but Jesus rescues us from the greatest threat the world has ever known: sin and death and hell. The pagan beliefs ran against everything the Jews believed, from promiscuity to idol worship, but in this very place, Jesus was proclaimed as Lord of all.

When we look around at the degradation of our culture and the poisonous language in our online communication, in families, and in politics, we can be deeply discouraged and furious, or we can remember that Jesus still rules and that Jesus still loves.

With this assurance, we can be agents of a love that surprises the people around us. Yes, we may disagree, but we love them anyway. Yes, we don't want to live like them, but we love them anyway. Yes, they've made tragic mistakes, but we love them anyway. This 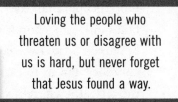 kind of love shouldn't be rare. It should be the norm for the family of God, among ourselves and as we relate to people outside the family.

Loving the people who threaten us or disagree with us is hard, but never forget that Jesus found a way.

What difference will it make to love them anyway?

- *A single individual* becomes an agent of change and a source of light. After all, it took the love of only one person, our Lord and Savior Jesus Christ, to turn the world upside down (in a good way).

- *A family* that loves this way has a mission, a cause, and a purpose to be salt to season and preserve their neighborhood. And this family will leave a legacy of love from generation to generation.

- *A small group* can work together to make a difference in the community, to be present as Jesus' hands, feet, and voice in the lives of people who have lost hope. Each person in the group brings unique talents and gifts.

- *A church community* can marshal their resources and work with other churches to provide ongoing services in their neighborhoods. They may start small, but if they catch God's heart, they'll find creative, bold ways to touch far more people than they could have imagined. It takes only one church with this loving spirit to launch a tidal wave of compassion as other churches join in to care for people throughout the city. The church will be a beacon of hope in the community and a resource to equip other churches to get involved in loving people others ignore.

Don't set your gaze on what's wrong with the world. That leads only to pride that we aren't like "them" and discouragement that we're losing ground. Instead, rivet your heart on Jesus. Embrace your assignment, which is the commission God has given you to love people who are hard to love.

You're already thinking about them. Don't wait. Love them today, and see how God uses you to change minds, hearts, and lives.

DISCUSSION QUESTIONS

- What are some instances when you've been surprised by love? Were you the recipient, the giver, or an onlooker? How did these moments affect you?

- What are some differences between seeing love as a growth strategy and seeing it as a lifestyle?

- What are some signs that we've designated a person or a group of people as "the other"?

- What needs to happen for us to see them—and treat them—as infinitely valuable because Jesus gave His life for them?

- Review Matthew 16:13–18. What difference does it make (or will it make) to fully grasp the truth that Jesus is King, even over the gates of hell and even in our divisive culture today?

- Describe your plan to fix your heart on Jesus, embrace your assignment, and love people who are hard to love.

ACTION POINT: WHAT LOVE LOOKS LIKE

God has probably put names and faces in your mind as you read this chapter. Every time I think of loving people—especially those who disagree with me and who think I don't belong—God reminds me of specific people who have hurt me. At these moments, you and I have a choice: we can ignore God's prompting to love them anyway, or we can move toward these people, listen until we understand their positions, empathize with their hearts, and treat them the way Jesus treated people—with love and truth.

Is this difficult? Yes. It calls us to dig far deeper into the love of God for us so His love flows out of us. I believe we learn to love by practicing love. As we reach out to love those people, it may be awkward at first, but God will gradually transform our hearts, our attitudes, and our ability to love them anyway.

This is a challenge for me every single day. But it's God's calling for me, and I'm determined to answer His call.

What about you? Will you join me and embrace your assignment to love them anyway?

USING *LOVE THEM ANYWAY* IN SMALL GROUPS AND CLASSES

THIS BOOK IS designed for individual study, small groups, and classes. The best way to absorb and apply these principles is for each person to individually study and answer the questions at the end of each chapter and then discuss them in either a class or a group environment.

Each chapter's questions are designed to promote reflection, application, and discussion. Be sure to order enough copies of *Love Them Anyway* for each person to have one. For couples, encourage both to have their own book so they can record their individual reflections.

Here's a recommended schedule for a small group or class:

Week 1

Introduce the material. As a group leader, share your hopes for the group, and provide books for each person. Encourage people to read the assigned chapter each week and answer the questions.

Weeks 2–11

Each week, introduce the topic for the week and share a story of how God has used Pastor Choco's principles in your life. In small groups, lead people through a discussion of the questions at the end of the chapter. In classes, teach the principles in each chapter, use personal illustrations, and invite discussion.

PERSONALIZE EACH LESSON

Ask people in the group to share their responses to the questions that meant the most to them that week. Make sure you personalize the principles and applications. At least once in each group meeting, add your own story to illustrate a particular point.

Make the Scriptures come alive. Far too often, we read the Bible like it's a phone book, with little or no emotion. Paint vivid pictures for people. Provide insights about the context of people's encounters with God, and help those in your class or group sense the emotions of specific people in each scene.

FOCUS ON APPLICATION

The questions at the end of each chapter and your encouragement to group members to be authentic will help your group take big steps to apply the principles they're learning. Share how you are applying the principles in particular chapters each week, and encourage the members of your group to take steps of growth too.

THREE TYPES OF QUESTIONS

If you have led groups for a few years, you already understand the importance of using open questions to stimulate discussion. Three types of questions are *limiting, leading,* and *open*. Many of the questions at the end of each lesson are open questions.

- Limiting questions focus on an obvious answer, such as, "What does Jesus call Himself in John 10:11?" They don't stimulate reflection or discussion. If you want to use questions like these, follow them with thought-provoking open questions.

- Leading questions require the listener to guess what the leader has in mind, such as, "Why did Jesus use the metaphor of a shepherd in John 10?" (He was probably alluding to a passage in Ezekiel, but many people don't know that.) The teacher who asks a leading question has a definite answer in mind. Instead of asking this kind of question, though, you should just teach the point and perhaps ask an open question about the point you have made.

- Open questions usually don't have right or wrong answers. They stimulate thinking and discussion, and they are far less threatening because the person answering doesn't risk ridicule for being wrong. These questions often begin with "Why do you think...?" or "What are some reasons that…?" or "How would you have felt in that situation?"

PREPARATION

As you prepare to teach this material in a group or class, consider these steps:

1. Carefully and thoughtfully read the book. Make notes, highlight key sections, quotes, or stories, and complete the discussion questions at the end of each chapter. This will familiarize you with the entire scope of the content.

2. As you prepare for each week's class or group, read the corresponding chapter again and make additional notes.

3. Tailor the amount of content to the time allotted. Encourage people to study the passages, and invite them to share what they've learned.

4. Add your own stories to personalize the message and add impact.

5. Before and during your preparation, ask God to give you wisdom, clarity, and power. Trust Him to use your group to change people's lives.

6. Remind your class that they will get far more out of the group if they read the chapter and complete the discussion questions each week.

ABOUT THE AUTHOR

WIDELY KNOWN AS "Pastor Choco," Wilfredo De Jesús is the founding pastor of New Life Covenant Church in Chicago. Under Pastor Choco's leadership, New Life Covenant became the largest Hispanic church in the Assemblies of God Fellowship. Today De Jesús serves in the Assemblies of God National Office as the general treasurer.

De Jesús was born and raised in Chicago's Humboldt Park community. When he was fourteen years old, he received Jesus as his Lord and Savior at a small Pentecostal Spanish-speaking church in the community. From that moment, his life was forever transformed.

He remained in that same little church for over twenty-three years before he was appointed senior pastor in July 2000 and the name of the church was changed to New Life Covenant Church. Since then, the church has grown from a weekly attendance of 120 to 17,000 globally through church plants and more than seventy-five ministries, many of which reach out to serve the most disenfranchised—the broken-hearted, poor, homeless, prostitutes, drug addicts, and gang members.

De Jesús has been instrumental in the development of several community-based programs such as the Chicago Master's Commission, an intensive discipleship program for college-age students, and the Chicago Dream Center, which offers various programs and services to assist individuals and families to move toward self-sufficiency and to overcome poverty and its ill effects.

De Jesús' vision is simple: to be a church for the hurting that reaches people for Jesus.

In 2012 De Jesús released his first book, *Amazing Faith*, in which he shares his life story and this key message: "No one is beyond the transforming power of God's love. When we let Him, God fills our hearts with His love, strength, and purpose, and we become complete." And in 2014 *In the Gap*—a book that describes what we can learn from the courage of nine heroes of the faith in the Scriptures—was published.

In April 2013 De Jesús was named one of *Time* magazine's one hundred most influential people in the world and recognized for his leadership and influence with evangelical and Latino audiences. He wants others to understand that his accomplishments are based on a life dedicated to God and God's purposes. In other words, whatever the accomplishment, to God be the glory! He has written two other books, *Stay the Course* and *Move Into More*.

De Jesús is a sought-after speaker at various church events, leadership conferences, and assemblies throughout the nation and abroad. He resides in Springfield, Missouri, with his wife, Elizabeth. They have three children, Alexandria, Yesenia, and Wilfredo Jr.; two sons-in-law, Anthony Gomez and Anders Hagstrom; one daughter-in-law, Eden De Jesús; and four pretty-amazing grandchildren, Charlie, Reagan, James, and Donovan.

NOTES

CHAPTER 1

1. Paul Delaney, "Looting, Vandalism Follow Chicago Riot," *New York Times,* June 6, 1977, https://www.nytimes.com/1977/06/06/archives/looting-vandalism-follow-chicago-riot-police-strength-stepped-up-in.html.
2. Frederick Lowe and Derrick Blakley, "2d Day of Humboldt Riots," *Chicago Tribune,* June 6, 1977.
3. Roberto Suro, "Humboldt Park: 'Community Without Dreams,'" *Chicago Tribune,* June 4, 1978.
4. "Verse-by-Verse Bible Commentary: Luke 15:8," StudyLight.org, accessed January 31, 2020, https://www.studylight.org/commentary/luke/15-8.html.
5. C. S. Lewis, *The Four Loves* (New York: HarperCollins, 1960), https://www.amazon.com/Four-Loves-C-S-Lewis/dp/0062565397/.

CHAPTER 2

1. Tobias Rose-Stockwell, "This Is How Your Fear and Outrage Are Being Sold for Profit," *Quartz,* July 28, 2017, https://qz.com/1039910/how-facebooks-news-feed-algorithm-sells-our-fear-and-outrage-for-profit/.
2. Arlie Russell Hochschild, *Strangers in Their Own Land: Anger and Mourning on the American Right* (New York: The New Press, 2016), 227, https://www.amazon.com/Strangers-Their-Own-Land-Mourning/dp/1620973499/.
3. Carroll Doherty, Jocelyn Kiley, and Bridget Johnson, "The Partisan Divide on Political Values Grows Even Wider," Pew Research Center, October 5, 2017, http://assets.pewresearch.org/wp-content/uploads/sites/5/2017/10/05162647/10-05-2017-Political-landscape-release.pdf.
4. Shanto Iyengar, Gaurav Sood, and Yphtach Lelkes, "Affect, Not Ideology: A Social Identity Perspective on Polarization," *Public Opinion Quarterly* 76, no. 3 (September 2012): 405–431, https://www.researchgate.net/publication/255992384_Affect_Not_Ideology_A_Social_Identity_Perspective_on_Polarization.

CHAPTER 3

1. Key Substance Use and Mental Health Indicators in the United States: Results from the 2018 National Survey on Drug Use and Health, Substance Abuse and Mental Health Services Administration, August 2019, 2, https://www.samhsa.gov/data/sites/default/files/cbhsq-reports/NSDUHNationalFindingsReport2018/NSDUHNationalFindingsReport2018.pdf.

2. Eric Stice et al., "An 8-Year Longitudinal Study of the Natural History of Threshold, Subthreshold, and Partial Eating Disorders from a Community Sample of Adolescents," *Journal of Abnormal Psychology*, 118, no. 3 (August 2009): 587–597, https://www.ncbi.nlm.nih.gov/pmc/articles/PMC2849679/.

3. "Facts and Statistics," Anxiety and Depression Association of America, accessed February 3, 2020, https://adaa.org/about-adaa/press-room/facts-statistics.

4. "Major Depression," National Institute of Mental Health, February 2019, https://www.nimh.nih.gov/health/statistics/major-depression.shtml.

5. "Get the Facts & Figures," The National Domestic Violence Hotline, accessed February 3, 2020, https://www.thehotline.org/resources/statistics/.

6. "Marriage and Divorce," American Psychological Association, accessed February 3, 2020, https://www.apa.org/topics/divorce/.

7. Miroslav Volf, *Exclusion and Embrace: A Theological Exploration of Identity, Otherness, and Reconciliation*, rev. ed. (Nashville: Abingdon Press, 2019), 125, https://www.amazon.com/Exclusion-Embrace-Revised-Updated-Reconciliation/dp/1501861077.

8. Volf, *Exclusion and Embrace*, 125.

9. Shahram Heshmat, "What Is Confirmation Bias?" *Psychology Today*, April 23, 2015, https://www.psychologytoday.com/us/blog/science-choice/201504/what-is-confirmation-bias.

10. During the writing of this book, I was elected general treasurer of the Assemblies of God National Office, so Elizabeth and I, with heavy hearts, have moved from Chicago to Springfield, Missouri, to follow God's call. That's the only reason we're willing to leave Humboldt Park—not for convenience, not for safety, not for better

prices for housing, but only in response to God's clear call. When we settled in Springfield, we looked for common ground instead of a battleground.

CHAPTER 4

1. David Brooks, "America Is Having a Moral Convulsion," *The Atlantic*, October 5, 2020, https://www.theatlantic. com/ideas/archive/2020/10/collapsing-levels-trust-are-devastating-america/616581/.
2. Samuel Moyn, "We're in an Anti-liberal Moment. Liberals Need Better Answers," *Washington Post*, June 21, 2019, https://www.washingtonpost.com/outlook/ were-in-an-anti-liberal-moment-liberals-need-better-answers/2019/06/21/5f276b26-91f7-11e9-b72d-d56510fa753e_story.html
3. David French, "Evangelicals Are Supporting Trump Out of Fear, Not Faith" *Time*, June 27, 2019, https://time. com/5615617/why-evangelicals-support-trump/.
4. Brené Brown, *Daring Greatly* (New York: Avery, 2012), 34, 37, https://www.google.com/books/edition/Daring_Greatly/2JFADwAAQBAJ.
5. Concepts on Jesus' vulnerability are taken from Timothy Keller, "Doing Justice and Mercy" (sermon, Redeemer Presbyterian Church, New York, March 20, 2016), https:// www.youtube.com/watch?v=u8Fn4vTTXHM.

CHAPTER 5

1. Martin Luther King Jr., "I Have a Dream" (speech, March on Washington for Jobs and Freedom, Washington, DC, August 28, 1963), https://kinginstitute.stanford.edu/king-papers/documents/i-have-dream-address-delivered-march-washington-jobs-and-freedom.

CHAPTER 6

1. Courtney Crowder and MacKenzie Elmer, "Postville Raid Anniversary: A Timeline of Events in One of America's Largest Illegal Immigration Campaigns," *Des Moines Register*, May 10, 2018, https://www.desmoinesregister. com/story/news/investigations/2018/05/10/postville-raid-anniversary-timeline-aaron-rubashkin-agriprocessors-postville-iowa-immigration-raid/588025002/.

2. Anthony Iaccarino, "The Founding Fathers and Slavery," *Encyclopaedia Britannica*, July 28, 2016, https://www.britannica.com/topic/The-Founding-Fathers-and-Slavery-1269536.
3. Quoted in "Timothy Keller on the Love of God," Redeemer Baptist Church, March 9, 2015, http://www.redeemerbc.org/blog/2015/3/8/tim-keller-on-the-love-of-god.
4. I'm sure you've noticed that I come back to the heart of the gospel in every chapter. This isn't an editing mistake. The gospel of grace is our only hope that God will transform us into people who love the way Jesus loves. We can never hear it too often because we will never get to the bottom of God's limitless love.

CHAPTER 7

1. Today some of those people are members of our church. They've come to Christ and left the homosexual lifestyle, and now they serve Jesus with freedom and joy.
2. Doug Stewart, "My Great-Great-Grandfather Hated the Gettysburg Address. 150 Years Later, He's Famous for It," *Smithsonian Magazine*, November 18, 2013, https://www.smithsonianmag.com/history/my-great-great-grandfather-hated-the-gettysburg-address-150-years-later-hes-famous-for-it-180947746/.

CHAPTER 8

1. John F. Walvoord, "Why I Believe the Bible," accessed February 7, 2020, https://walvoord.com/article/316.

CHAPTER 9

1. "Chicago Pizza Delivery Woman Moved to Tears After Church Honors Her With Incredible Tip," WGN, March 2, 2018, https://wgntv.com/2018/03/02/chicago-pizza-delivery-woman-moved-to-tears-after-church-honors-her-with-incredible-tip/.
2. Quentin Fortrell, "People Spend Most of Their Waking Hours Staring at Screens," MarketWatch, August 4, 2018, https://www.marketwatch.com/story/people-are-spending-most-of-their-waking-hours-staring-at-screens-2018-08-01.
3. Catriona Harvey-Jenner, "The Psychology of a Like: How Social Media Is Really Affecting Your Brain," *Cosmopolitan*,

July 25, 2017, https://www.cosmopolitan.com/uk/reports/
a9931660/psychology-social-media-likes-mental-health-
issues/.

4. Rebecca Webber, "The Comparison Trap," *Psychology Today*,
November 7, 2017, https://www.psychologytoday.com/us/
articles/201711/the-comparison-trap.

5. Matthew Shaer, "What Emotion Goes Viral the
Fastest?" *Smithsonian Magazine*, April 2014, https://www.
smithsonianmag.com/science-nature/what-emotion-goes-
viral-fastest-180950182/

6. Susanna Schrobsdorff, "The Rage Flu: Why All This Anger
Is Contagious and Making Us Sick," *Time*, June 29, 2017,
https://time.com/4838673/anger-and-partisanship-as-a-
virus/.

7. To see a graph of the bias of news outlets, go to https://
www.adfontesmedia.com/static-mbc/?v=402f03a963ba.

8. "Dehydrated? How Not Drinking Enough Water Impacts
Your Eyes," Essilor News, accessed February 7, 2020,
https://www.essilorusa.com/newsroom/dehydrated-how-not-
drinking-enough-water-impacts-your-eyes.

DESTROY WALLS THAT DIVIDE US.

I'm so happy you read my book. I hope it has encouraged you to redirect your passion, refine your purpose, and see God use you in ways you never imagined.

AS MY WAY OF SAYING THANK YOU, I AM OFFERING YOU A FREE GIFT:

- **Everlasting Hope**: *Inspirational Messages That Encourage, Motivate, and Heal in Any Situation*

**To get this
FREE GIFT, please go to:**

lovethembook.com/gift

Thanks again and God bless you,

Choco De Jesús

CHARISMA
HOUSE